Language Knowledge for Primary Teachers

A Guide to Textual, Grammatical and Lexical Study

Angela Wilson

David Fulton Publishers

London

David Fulton Publishers Ltd
Ormond House, 26–27 Boswell Street, London WC1N 3JZ

www.fultonpublishers.co.uk

First edition published in Great Britain by David Fulton Publishers 1999
Reprinted 2000 (twice)
Second edition published in Great Britain by David Fulton Publishers 2001

British Library Cataloguing in Publication Data
A catalogue record for this book is available from the British Library

ISBN 1–85346–753–7

Typeset by FiSH Books, London
Printed in Great Britain by The Cromwell Press Ltd, Trowbridge, Wilts.

Contents

For Andrew
and
For Isobel

Acknowledgements

There are no right ways to prepare people to become primary teachers: only an apparently endless series of painful choices. I would like to thank all my students who over the years have borne with my attempts to get it right, and my colleagues, who have endured, more or less cheerfully, my suggestions that we try things a little differently, yet again. I can't promise that there is an end in sight.

I am very grateful to all the students, colleagues and friends who have contributed in various ways to the production of this book. I would especially like to thank my husband and my sister. Given all the other demands there are on time, I don't think I would have persisted but for their encouragement.

I would like to thank the publishers, authors and colleagues who have been kind enough to grant permission for material to be reprinted: in particular, John Dixon and Irene Farmer for 'Fred at the Zoo'; Hodder & Stoughton Educational for an extract from *Living Language: Exploring Advanced Level English Language* by Keith and Shuttleworth; Multilingual Matters Ltd for 'My Language is my Home' by Pirkko Leporanta-Morley, quoted in *Minority Education* by Skutnabb-Kangas and Cummins; Kit Wright for *The Frozen Man*.

Auditing your language knowledge – doing it yourself

Before starting to use this book, you may find it useful to take stock of your language knowledge – to undertake a 'self audit', as the current jargon has it. If you think that this would be helpful, you will find some language activities and accompanying commentaries in Appendix 1 on p.153.

Introduction

Who is this book for?

In writing this book I had two audiences in mind. The first group is student teachers. The second includes all those primary teachers in all parts of the British Isles who are trying to implement multi-strategy approaches to literacy, but perhaps especially those who are trying to implement the National Literacy Strategy.

The wider educational context

The book has been written in the context of two recent government initiatives. One is the National Literacy Strategy and the other is the National Curriculum for Initial Teacher Training (ITT) (DfEE Circular 04/98) which, in the section referring to English, 'specifies the essential core of knowledge, understanding and skills which all primary trainees, on all courses of initial teacher training, must be taught and be able to use ...' (Annex C, p.1). The document is in three sections. It is the third section on students' own knowledge and understanding of English which has caused the most concern amongst student teachers and teacher trainers because the document specifies a very detailed body of knowledge to be acquired by students at lexical, grammatical and textual levels. All teacher training institutions are required to carry out audits of their students' knowledge at each of these levels and have been told that 'only those trainees who have shown that they have the knowledge, understanding and skills to teach effectively are judged to have successfully completed a course leading to Qualified Teacher Status' (Annex C, p.1).

The current situation

Teacher training courses are always crowded, even the three- or four-year ones. PGCEs are phenomenally so. Some of the students who are accepted on to teacher training courses are unsure of their grasp of the forms of language, whether written or spoken. Very few in recent years have had much teaching at school on the structures of the English language at any level. In tackling the requirements of this new legislation many new entrants to courses at present feel as though they are starting from a low baseline. The language audits that we have carried out at my own college show that this is indeed the case.

Possible ways forward

Is this language knowledge really necessary? Public anxiety about standards of speaking, reading and writing seems to be a permanent feature of national life, but there is no reputable research evidence to suggest that the preparation of students to teach English in primary schools has been seriously flawed in recent years. It is true to say that emphasis has largely been placed on the 'process' aspects of language, that is to say on encouraging students – and children in schools – to read widely and to speak and write for a wide range of audiences and purposes. Possibly not enough attention has been paid to what a speaker or writer needs to know about language in order to take part in a speech event, or to put a written text together. Perhaps there was too facile an assumption sometimes that knowledge about speaking and writing would be picked up 'on the wing', as it were. Reading instruction too tended to come to a halt once readers had gained the 'independence' stage. With the right kinds of support, many readers might be willing to see interesting possibilities in more complex texts.

The key words here are 'with the right kinds of support'. The difficulty with the ITT National Curriculum is that it presents items of language knowledge to be acquired by student teachers without any accompanying rationale for how they are to make use of it once they are in the classroom. It's as if to know what a digraph is, or a subordinate clause, is indisputably 'a good thing'. Knowledge of any kind is not much use to the knower unless it fits into some existing pattern in the mind. In the case of intending primary teachers, the language knowledge must fit into their thinking about how to help children in primary classrooms enjoy their encounters with language, and to become more confident, enthusiastic and competent readers, writers and speakers. Presented as separate items of knowledge to be 'mugged up' in order to get past the audit, the language knowledge will soon be forgotten or, just as bad, passed on to children in the same meaningless way as a series of decontextualised language activities.

The role of English/language in the curriculum

It is vitally important that student teachers develop their understanding of the place of language in our culture and in the social groups in which each of us operates. They must know what it means to be literate in a late twentieth-century context, with new technologies offering wider experiences of reading alongside the undiminished pleasures of traditional kinds. They must have some insight into the skills and achievements of writers, with a special emphasis on those who write with children in mind. But also they must understand the importance of language, whether in written or spoken mode, for the children they teach, in discovering their sense of self and their relationships with the world around them. These are the areas with which the subject 'English' has concerned itself for some years now and it must go on doing so. All this may seem rather complex and nebulous compared with learning ten facts about 'the verb' for an end of term audit, but in the long run it is the latter which will turn out to have been a waste of time unless teachers can relate it to the wider picture of English teaching which I have outlined here. And I think it can be done. I hope that this book will begin to show how.

The National Literacy Strategy

For teachers already in primary schools, the situation is in some ways similar. I am thinking particularly now of those teachers who are implementing the National Literacy Strategy, in Key Stage 2 especially. They have been presented with a formidable list of learning objectives at text, sentence and word levels. Although some in-service help is available, many teachers, like the students, feel that at present they are starting from a low knowledge base as regards some aspects of the work. There is perhaps a tendency to 'cherry pick' those bits of the strategy which seem most manageable. It's a complex document and it can be read in a variety of ways. Sections of the press have chosen to hail it as a return to phonics, for example. Taken as a whole, with each level of language carefully linked to the others, it can sustain and support that view of the true concerns of English teaching which I outlined above. I hope that this book will help primary teachers by supplementing the in-service support that is available, and by giving some underpinning to the framework document.

My language is my home

In my mother tongue my
hatred is sanguineous,
my love soft.

My innermost soul
is in balance
with my language.
The closeness of it
caresses my hair.

It has grown
together with me,
has taken roots in me.

My language
can be painted over
but not detached
without tearing
the structure of my cells.

If you paint a foreign language
on my skin
my innermost soul
cannot breathe.

The glow of my feelings
will not get through
the blocked pores.

There will be
a burning fever
rising for a way
to express itself.

Pirkko Leporanta-Morley,
quoted in Skutnabb-Kangas and Cummins (1988)

Chapter 1

Why do primary teachers need language knowledge?

A student in tears is a depressing sight. From time to time, towards the beginning of the academic year – say in mid-October – a woe-begone first year may be found hovering around at the end of a lecture, when everyone else has gone. After paper hankies and a sympathetic ear have been provided, it emerges that the student is upset because she has been asked to produce a piece of writing – a story, let's say – and later on, to share her first draft with a fellow student with a view to developing it further. So far, it isn't too difficult to understand her anxieties, but sometimes I have found that the next statement stretches sympathy to the utmost. It goes something like this: 'I want to work with little ones and I came on to a primary course because I thought I would only have to teach them sentences and where to put full stops and capital letters.'

Now thankfully these episodes are fairly unusual; only one or two people have gone so far as to reconsider their career choices. But their stories raise some interesting issues. This is a book about language knowledge: the kinds of knowledge about language primary teachers need in order to do their job successfully. We all acquire language knowledge as part of living our lives: we listen, we talk, we read, we write. Some of us do more of these things than others, and the kinds of listening, speaking, reading and writing we do will vary enormously. But what should parents, children, governors, OFSTED inspectors and others expect of us as teachers who have been through a course of professional training? One obvious way of beginning to think about this question might be to turn to the National Curriculum.[1]

The requirements of the National Curriculum

The programmes of study for speaking, listening, reading and writing set out the legal requirements for what children must learn. Even the most cursory glance at the programmes of study for writing at Key Stage 1 should have convinced my sad students that a great deal more is required than composing isolated sentences and learning to punctuate them correctly.

Pupils should be taught to vary their writing to suit the purpose and reader. They should be taught to write in a range of forms, incorporating some of the different characteristics of those forms. The range should include narratives, notes, lists, captions, records, messages, instructions. (p.49)

By the time we reach Key Stage 2, the list includes:

- playscripts
- reports
- explanations
- opinions
- reviews
- commentaries.

(p.58)

At Key Stage 2 pupils are required to use features of layout, presentation and organisation effectively. The programmes of study for speaking and listening, and for reading, make it equally clear that children must become skilled practitioners of language in these modes also.

The present government (1998) has set a target of 80 per cent of all 11-year-olds having reached Level 4, as measured by standard assessment tests (SATs), by 2002.[2]

In reading, this includes being able to:

- respond to a range of texts, showing understanding of significant ideas, themes, events and characters
- locate ideas and information in reading non-fiction texts.

There is no external test for speaking and listening. They are assessed by teachers. In this mode of language, pupils who have reached Level 4 should be able to:

- talk and listen with confidence in an increasing range of contexts
- adapt their talk according to its purpose
- develop ideas thoughtfully
- describe events
- convey their opinions clearly
- listen carefully
- make contributions and ask questions that are responsive to others' ideas and views
- use appropriately some of the features of standard English vocabulary and grammar.

Language as process; language as product

It's not easy to digest the fine detail of government documents. The reader's eye tends to slide over it, trying to get at the main drift. If you are prepared to go back more carefully, however, over what has been quoted above, you might be able to detect statements about language of two contrasting kinds. These are examples of the first kind:

- help children to vary their writing to suit the purpose and the reader
- help them to become responsive readers, exploring ideas, themes, events and characters in the texts they encounter
- encourage them to become enthusiastic and confident talkers.

I am making a selection from the quotations above in order to stress the process aspects of language work. What I have in mind is that we can envisage a class-room where children are using language to understand the world better, including the world of reading and the media, and are finding in language ways to explore their own feelings and attitudes towards what these worlds portray. These children will create in response to their thinking and feeling a range of texts, both written and spoken, which will bring pleasure and delight to themselves, their teachers, parents and others. The talking, the reading and the writing will flow out, across the whole curriculum and even beyond it.

Yet if I make another selection from my original quotations, I can present a different picture, much more oriented towards language as product or social system. This time, the National Curriculum is urging teachers to:

- show children how to organise and present their writing in different ways
- ensure that they incorporate into their writing 'some characteristics of the various forms'
- show understanding of ideas (instead of 'explore ideas')
- ensure that children are taught the grammatical constructions that are charac-teristic of spoken standard English and to apply this knowledge appropriately in a range of contexts.

In this second selection we have language work seen not so much as process, or ways of getting things done, but as a system, or set of rules, external to the child and which the child must learn and adopt.

Where does the teacher's duty lie?

Teachers want to be accountable to their various publics – the children, the parents, the head teacher, the local education authority (LEA) and so on. But they may find themselves trying to cope with conflicting views of language work both within and between these various groups. Does the teacher's prime responsibility lie with accepting the language the child brings from home and providing opportunities to use that language in a rich and varied selection of contexts? This would be to emphasise the process approach. Or does it rather lie with presenting, in a carefully planned series of stages, all those aspects of the language system with which children may still be unfamiliar when they come to school? Is one approach (the first) perhaps more appropriate in Key Stage 1, while the second might fit better into a Key Stage 2 programme?

Let me remind you that it was I who separated these two sets of quotations into what I have labelled 'process' and 'system', or 'product.' *Both* are to be found in the National Curriculum. My experience, however, accords with that of the Bullock Report, when as long ago as 1975 the committee pointed out that 'where a teacher subscribes to a particular approach, he [sic] does not necessarily pursue it exclusively, neglecting everything else. Nevertheless, emphases do exist and there is a tendency to oversimplify processes which are in fact very complex' (p.4). I don't think that the advent of the National Curriculum changed that very much. Even though, as I have illustrated, that document unites both the process and the systems approaches, nevertheless many teachers have in practice continued to emphasise one or the other, 'process' *or* 'product'. I think it is true to say that many practising teachers' own language knowledge is predominantly of one kind or the other.

'Pupil-centred' vs. 'social needs' approaches to language

The process approach to language has often been described as 'pupil-centred'. Often unfairly, but sometimes justifiably, it has come under attack for being too *laissez-faire*, and for lacking rigour, not setting sufficiently high standards for language work. You will probably be familiar with terms such as 'progressive methods' being bandied about in the media, often with very little attempt to define or justify them. It has suited politicians of all persuasions to keep alive anxieties about standards, especially in literacy, and to blame these so-called 'progressive methods' for a decline. Put very crudely, this tends to result in a shift away from concerns for pupils as individual language users towards some more external view of 'the needs of society' which the pupils must be educated to serve. Recent government documents, particularly the National Literacy Strategy and the National Curriculum for Initial Teacher Training (ITT) could be seen as giving a very hefty push indeed towards language as social system, rather than language as process. If this goes too far, we are in danger of reducing language to a set of facts to be learned and usages to be practised. The enthusiasm for talking, reading and writing which comes from feeling confident about 'having a go' could well be sacrificed. We come back to the importance of reading the small print, of coping with the detail and not just the drift of recent legislation. I believe that each of the recent documents provides scope for primary teachers to hold on to a view of language which stresses the paramount importance of turning children into confident and skilled readers, writers and speakers, who can make the complexities of the language system serve their needs, and not the other way round.

Uniting process and product

What kinds of language knowledge would teachers need to bring this about? First and foremost they need to ensure that the language knowledge they acquire, whether as part of their training or outside it, is used to develop them, the teachers, as skilled language practitioners. Only then can they hope to foster those skills and the enthusiasm for language and confidence in engaging with it that children need. This may seem a tall order. Many students who embark on a course of teacher training do not come to college with a subject strength in English. The time they have available for studying English is relatively limited. Reading, let alone writing, may not be a favourite leisure time occupation. However, before any more students are reduced to tears, let me explain a little more about what I mean.

Reading a wide variety of texts

As far as reading is concerned, for example, being a skilled practitioner does not mean engaging with the canon of English literature. (Though there are those who might see this as desirable. Heavens, there are even those who see it as enjoyable.) It does mean reading widely from a range of types of text such as are set out in the National Literacy Strategy (1998). This document includes fiction, poetry and non-fiction. It is not widely used in Wales, but students in Welsh colleges would nevertheless find the range of text types set out there a very useful starting point for developing their own reading.[3]

As you read, you need to develop your awareness of what Jonathan Culler (1975) calls the 'possibilities of literature'. This means, for example, being prepared to see a writer as someone who has some skill in constructing a text, someone who has chosen a word or a sentence with great care for the impact it might have on the reader. This applies just as much in the case of those who write non-fiction and those who write primarily with children in mind. In fact, many writers whose work ends up being enjoyed by children did *not* write primarily with them in mind. C.S. Lewis, for example, makes the point that it just happens that the things he liked writing were the things children liked reading. Of course, writers can never be sure of the effect their words will have on the readers. People who read a lot have more and more reading experience to bring to bear each time they read, as well as a mass of other experience they acquire in life generally. This will inevitably lead to the text being to some extent created anew in the mind of every reader each time it is read, though it would be surprising if people who share a culture did not frequently find a large measure of agreement about their responses to a book.[4]

You may be surprised and perhaps a little daunted by these comments on reading, especially if you embarked on becoming a teacher with the idea that reading was something to do with turning sounds into written symbols or vice versa. Of course, that is also a vital part of the process. I shall try to show the relationship between the various aspects of the reading process in later chapters.

Creating spoken and written texts

Being a skilled practitioner also means having the confidence to have a go at creating texts yourself – for a variety of purposes and audiences. It means pushing your speaking skills into what are possibly new areas for you, such as modelling for the children the role of a doctor's receptionist in the home corner which has been transformed into a surgery for the week, or reading aloud with enough enthusiasm and skill to hold a class spellbound. These are just a few examples. Why are they so important? It's because if you can successfully turn yourself into a confident practitioner you have some hope of retaining a clear grasp of what language is for. Above all, language is for making and sharing meanings. Sometimes these meanings need to be available quickly and easily, as in a recipe or a railway timetable or giving someone directions to the railway station. Sometimes it's interesting to have to tease out the meaning from a piece of text, as frequently happens when we are reading a poem or a story. It may be that the writer is playing a joke on us – having fun with meaning. This is hugely enjoyable for all concerned. On some occasions, readers and listeners know that they are being given a biased view of events. We have all offered one ourselves when it suited our purposes.

It isn't just the content of the message, however, that is useful or enjoyable. Often, the way in which the content is presented is just as important. We have all felt cross with ourselves when we have messed up the telling of a joke or a shaggy dog story, and the whole effect is lost. In reading poetry, it is often the sound of the words that moves us as much as the message contained in them. There may be no message at all, when the writer is just having fun with sounds or with nonsense words. Or let us take a more down-to-earth example. Supposing we hope to impress an employer by the clarity of a report we have written, or persuade a bank manager to part with some cash. Certainly meanings need to come across clearly, but especially in these last two examples we need to choose that style of writing or speaking that we have seen described in the National Curriculum as standard English. These activities, which we are engaging in because we hope to profit from them, are a far cry from the fun of gossiping with friends and making them laugh as we turn the day's disasters into a funny story, perhaps drawing on a shared regional dialect.

Confident practitioners are willing to engage in all these activities and more. They embark on them with enthusiasm, expecting to receive profit or pleasure from them. They may find some of them difficult, but they know where to go for help. They are not afraid of making mistakes, but know how to set about correcting them. Teachers, as much as, or perhaps more than, any other group in society, need to be confident practitioners because they must fire children with their confidence and their enthusiasm.

Becoming a reflective language teacher

I have admitted that all this reading and writing, speaking and listening may seem a tall order. Yet there is more. The processes of speaking, reading and writing are not by themselves the whole story. Teachers need other kinds of language knowledge, knowledge of language as system, so that they can reflect on these activities, encouraging interactions with texts in a way that deepens knowledge and enjoyment. Vygotsky (1962) said that there are two stages in the development of knowledge. In the first stage we learn about things, or how to do things, but we don't know that we know these things. In the second stage there is a gradual increase in active, conscious control over the knowledge. (We begin to know what we know, and that there is more that we do not know.) From very early on in the process of developing children's literacy, teachers must help children to move into a more reflective stance towards language, which they can only do if they themselves are reflective readers and writers and speakers. So teachers must be people who talk about what they are reading, and help children to do the same. They must respond sensitively to a piece of children's writing, sharing with the child their enthusiasm for the child's achievement and perhaps suggesting areas for further work. After a role play is over, they will take a class through what has been said, highlighting especially interesting sections and discussing places where things could have been done differently.[5]

Can language be explicitly taught?

We have two kinds of language knowledge to consider: the kind that allows us to be what I have called 'skilled practitioners', and a related, but different, kind which allows us to talk about these practices, to analyse them, to highlight strengths and weaknesses. Sometimes, the first kind of language knowledge is called 'implicit'. People who use this term almost seem to suggest that this knowledge comes instinctively, from within us. Of course, this is obviously nonsense in one sense. None of us comes into the world able to speak or read or write. A very impressive amount of learning goes on at home, supported by parents and all those who form part of a child's early years. It is the task of teachers to take the child on from what has already been achieved.

The difficult question is, *how* do they do this? Does the language children bring with them to school go on developing mainly because they are given lots of opportunities to speak, to read and to write, with models of skilled practice to help them? Or is it helpful to children to be provided with some more explicit language knowledge? There are loud sounds of cans of worms opening at this point. To what extent can teachers, by talking about language explicitly, as a phenomenon to be 'put under the microscope', help children to become better practitioners?

As lecturers on courses of teacher training are fond of saying at difficult moments, 'It depends'. It depends, for example, on the individual. There are undoubtedly those children who acquire a sense of the possibilities of literature, or absorb new ways of saying things, or experiment with producing kinds of texts which they haven't written before, largely as a result of observing others and joining in with what they are doing. Yet perhaps we overestimate the numbers of those who can do this comfortably. Let me return briefly, for example, to the student I described at the beginning of this chapter. I assumed that she had acquired sufficient knowledge of stories from reading them and sharing them with others to be able to produce one herself. Plenty of models of stories are available from babyhood onwards and I had offered some models in previous lectures before asking the group to write. Yet even the keen reader of stories or teller of stories may struggle to construct something on paper. It doesn't just flow from the pen. In my own defence, let me remind you that I didn't assume that it did. That was my reason for suggesting a 'response partner' – a sympathetic fellow student who might be able to make helpful suggestions. There are, of course, social issues here. How well do we need to know someone before they can fulfil this role for us? But let's focus on the language issues. I, the lecturer, was now asking the students to find a vocabulary for making explicit the strengths and weaknesses of each other's stories. Of course, this need not involve very technical words: 'I think you need to say more about why he did that' doesn't require any specialised language vocabulary. Yet it shows some understanding of story structure. Someone with a bit more explicit language knowledge might have put it thus: 'The story isn't working because you need to build up this character a bit more.' It might be at the sentence level that a story is failing. We then need a reader whose ear has learned to respond to a faulty rhythm: 'Your sentences are a bit short. You need to join some of them together to make it flow a bit better. But leave that one short because it makes that part of your story sound really exciting.' In a stimulating language environment the next step might be for the writer to ask, 'How can I join them?' This might be the appropriate time for some direct input from a teacher: 'You need a wider range of conjunctions. You only seem to use "and" and "then".'

A language for talking about language

What we are seeing now is how language knowledge can be made explicit by means of a metalanguage – a language for talking about language. There is quite a lot of it in all the government documents I have mentioned so far, and it can seem alienating. Do primary teachers need to know what a conjunction is, or a text type, an affix, a simile, or a metaphor? We all use them, but do we need to label them, or talk about them? Any group of people who want to perfect their craft or hobby or interest – be it horse racing or photography or growing chrysanthemums – find themselves becoming more absorbed in the vocabulary of their subject. It helps them to become more precise, to talk more specifically about what they know or want to find out. In a sense, it helps them to see more clearly, to become more discriminating. At first when they join a club, those in the know seem frighteningly 'expert'. Yet their interest and enthusiasm usually overcomes the newcomer's feelings of anxiety and inadequacy. If we see explicit language knowledge in this light, it is surely a good thing. A class who have, with their teacher's encouragement, learnt to talk more precisely about what they or others are discussing, reading and writing are not going to be afraid of language, or of metalanguage, but will use it to build their knowledge and interest.

There is, of course, a social as well as a language aspect to what is going on at the photography lecture or the chrysanthemum society. Technical terms representing explicit knowledge of all kinds can be used to shore up the expert's sense of superiority, to signify power or status within a group, to slam the door in the face of slow learners or ones lacking in confidence. Then it becomes a bad thing.

Providing a context for language knowledge

There is a danger of explicit knowledge about language becoming divorced from practice, becoming an end in itself. This was certainly the case in my own school days, and it has given explicit language teaching a negative history. I didn't find it difficult, as it happened, to 'spot the metaphor in line ten', or even to divide complex sentences into clauses and write them in columns in my English book. But it was presented to us in such a way that it didn't seem to have any connection with our own reading and writing. (Speaking wasn't considered at all in those days.) And gradually, as those of us who enjoyed English grew up and became English teachers ourselves, we became convinced of the truth of this hypothesis: 'There was little or no connection', we said, 'between teaching about clauses and metaphors and the like and helping our pupils to become better readers and writers and speakers. So we had better stop wasting everybody's time and place the emphasis much more on language processes – reading a wider range of texts, writing for more purposes and for audiences other than the teacher, providing an opportunity for talk of all kinds to flourish in the classroom.'[6]

To some extent, we threw the baby out with the bath water. Of course, there are teachers who have gone on providing language activities which involve ruling columns in exercise books, writing lists of pronouns, answering questions on a piece of writing taken out of its context and reproduced in a book of comprehension exercises. They have produced generations of pupils who did these activities with varying degrees of success, but often remained unchanged by them. These teachers have helped to sustain the negative history I spoke about – to bring it into the present day. It need not be like this.

Can language teaching inform language using?

The challenge for tomorrow's teachers is to develop and to share language knowledge with their pupils in such a way that their explicit teaching informs and strengthens the children's practice. This is by no means easy to achieve. Should the explicit teaching be offered systematically, according to a preordained programme? The National Literacy Strategy has gone down this path, with its yearly and termly objectives. It runs the grave risk, though I'm sure this was not the intention, of returning teachers and children to a more sophisticated version of the decontextualised language work I deplored. Yet if we abandon the systematic approach, do we not run the risk of children's language knowledge being patchy at best? To meet this anxiety requires some very careful planning and record keeping on the part of teachers.

Language study as an end in itself

Presented by an enthusiastic and skilful teacher, language knowledge is also interesting in its own right, even though there may not always be an immediate practical application of it. Some work done on word derivation, for example, can be an interesting activity for its own sake. Good teaching about the way words develop and change can help to engender an interest in vocabulary, and in the long run this will probably enrich a child's reading and writing and speaking. It might also help with some spelling difficulties.

Wray and Medwell (1998, p.9) warn that learning is a situated process:

> Why is it that a child who spells ten words correctly in a spelling test is likely to spell several of them wrongly when writing a story a short while afterwards? The answer is simply that the learning of the spelling is so inextricably bound up with the context of the learning that it cannot easily be applied outside of this context.

Not easily, no, but it *can* be applied. The activities would be better presented the other way round. The child has a go at using a new word or words in writing a story, perhaps after meeting the words in a shared reading context and discussing their origins and meanings with the teacher. If the words are spelt wrongly, then the teacher can make links with the previous experience: 'Do you remember when we came across this word in shared reading? We said that it belongs to the ——— family. They all come from a shared root, ———.' The words generated from the children's writing can then go on to be part of the spelling test. Teachers and children will share an increasing number and range of learning contexts as a school year progresses, and it is an important part of a teacher's job to help children to make links from one context to another.

Finding a new way forward

Recent government documents, in particular the National Literacy Strategy and the National Curriculum for ITT, can give the impression of turning the clock back, of demanding the kinds of language knowledge from teachers and from children which some schools have resolutely turned away from for over 40 years or more. The effect on new entrants to courses of teacher training could be similar to that on the timid member of the chrysanthemum society. Feelings of alienation, of fear even, could rise strongly to the surface. Then acquiring knowledge about parts of speech, syntactic patterns, text types and so on can all too easily become ends in themselves. I hope that in subsequent chapters of this book I can help student teachers to develop the language knowledge they need in order to become sensitive and confident teachers so that language work becomes both an interesting study in its own right but, more importantly, provides a series of searchlights, to borrow a metaphor from the National Literacy Strategy, to help us all to find further ways of developing children's reading, writing and speaking.

Chapter 2

A framework for considering language knowledge

In Chapter 1 I introduced the concepts of language as process and language as product or system. I urged you to see it as vitally important to your work as primary teachers to increase your own confidence and skills in the processes of language. I hope I have said enough to convince you of how important this is and that you have already started to explore some writing for children which is new to you as well as writing something of your own!

In most of the subsequent chapters of this book I shall be mainly concerned with aspects of the language system, though always in the context of exploring how knowing more about the system might help in becoming a more informed and reflective practitioner. In the arrangement of the chapters I have adopted the three-part framework which you can also find in the National Literacy Strategy:

• what do primary teachers need to know about texts, and how they are constructed?
• what should they know about the rules of syntax and punctuation?
• what should they know about using vocabulary?

Starting from texts

If we want children to become informed and enthusiastic speakers, readers and writers, I believe that we must start with texts, making them and sharing them. Something happens when we become immersed in the meaning of a text which goes beyond the study of isolated words or sentences. Outside the confines of a linguistics department of a university there are few of us who find the prospect of studying the uses of the -ing participle, or the phoneme /ʃ/ more enticing than, for example, the following:

Chapter 1

THE BEAM OF DARKNESS

Here is Kate Tranter coming home from school in the January dusk – the first to come because she is the youngest of her family. Past the churchyard. Past the shops. Along the fronts of the tall, narrow terrace houses she goes. Not this one, nor this one, nor this ....

Stop at the house with no lit window.

This is home.

(Pearce 1983)

I am not claiming that it will necessarily be narrative that will engage every reader's interest. The kinds of enjoyment to be had from reading texts, and the range of uses too, are almost limitless and it has been exciting over the last few years to see the exclusive emphasis on story reading, and story writing, widening in primary schools. Some readers' attention will be attracted by an opening like this:

WHAT WERE DINOSAURS?

What would it have been like to have lived when dinosaurs ruled the earth? No book can really show you. You have to use your imagination. Imagine the ground shaking under your feet as a herd of 10,000 Triceratops stampedes towards you. Imagine the sound of a five-tonne duckbill dinosaur calling to his mate with its long, trombone-like head crest. Imagine the sight and smell of a herd of 40-tonne Brachiosaurus in a conifer forest, pine needles showering down from their munching mouths, 14 metres above you. (Theodorou 1995)

Texts, whether written or spoken, offer us opportunities to indulge our interests – to gossip about the neighbours, or find out more about life in England as Jane Austen saw it, or about how to grow chrysanthemums for that matter.

How are texts constructed?

The aim of primary English teaching must be to help pupils to become more powerful participators in text making and text sharing. But for this to happen, they must delve into language below the text level, must find out more about how the resources of the language enable us to package and present meaning in interesting and varied ways. Children can be shown how writers learn to exploit the possibilities of syntax, that is, the rules for constructing sentences for a range of purposes. Words can be used literally or figuratively. They don't just label aspects of experience but bring with them a wealth of cultural, social and personal associations. And those words are built up from the 44 or so phonemes which comprise the sounds of English. Learning about the graphemes, or combinations of letters of the alphabet which enable those sounds to be written down, may help children to get to grips with aspects of the writing system.

The National Literacy Strategy: too many objectives?

I am sketching out simply the bare bones of a framework for knowledge about the language system. In recent months the National Literacy Strategy has put some very detailed flesh indeed on those bones, at least as regards the teaching of reading and writing. There are frequently a dozen or more learning objectives for each term in the word level columns of the National Literacy Strategy, almost as many in the sentence sections, and 20 plus in the text level work. There is considerable overlap from term to term, but nevertheless this represents a formidable body of content, especially for non-specialist primary teachers. There is a danger of teachers being deskilled by this highly directive document, of being put in the position of 'delivering' the literacy hour, without any real understanding of its rationale. As Elizabeth Plackett says (1998, p.7): this could lead to some very boring and monotonous teaching. 'Unless teachers have a good understanding of the underlying rationale for an approach, over time it will inevitably become diluted and increasingly mechanical. It seems axiomatic that an approach which emphasises the importance of children reflecting on their own learning also demands reflective teachers.'

Elizabeth Plackett's last words here, about the importance of reflective teachers, provide a useful point for you to pause in your reading, if you will, and do a little bit of reflecting yourselves. In this book, you are being asked to consider language as a 'three-tiered system' of texts, sentences and words, and I am further making the claim that the text level is the place where all thinking about language should start, with sentence and word level knowledge developing from text making and sharing. This would be my starting point in any primary classroom, as much in Reception as in Year 6.

'Top-down' or 'bottom-up' approaches to language work?

There is some evidence to suggest that there is a tension in government circles between opposing points of view about the amount of importance to be given to text level work. In the framework document the learning objectives are arranged in columns, with word level work placed in the position that the eye naturally goes to first, on the left-hand side of the page. This seems to suggest that teachers should start with work at that level. Yet the famous (or infamous) 'literacy clock' which sets out how the literacy hour is to be divided up, starts with 15 minutes' worth of shared reading of a text, from which teachers are encouraged to build their word and sentence level work. You may think that my suspicions spring from no more than a fanciful reaction to some page lay out, but the ITT National Curriculum states with no ambiguity:

as part of all courses trainees must be taught about the emphasis that should be given to teaching at each level [*by which they mean word, sentence or text level*] depending on pupils' ages and the stage of their development in English, *e.g. giving greatest attention to teaching word level skills to beginning readers.*

(The Teacher Training Agency 1998, Annex C, p.4)

What do you think?

How do you think work on the language system should be introduced in the primary school? Does effective language work, whether we are thinking about literacy or oracy (speaking and listening) start from texts and work down from there to studying the smaller units of language? This could be described as a 'top-down approach'. Or is the reverse more effective, especially perhaps in Key Stage 1 – a 'bottom-up approach'? This would emphasise, in the early years at least, an emphasis on decoding and encoding letters and words. I believe that your answer to this question will have considerable bearing on the kinds of language knowledge that you feel you need as a primary teacher – in other words, on what you are looking for as you read this book. Until you are clear about that, it may be a waste of time to proceed.

> Unless it grows out of yourself
>   No knowledge is really yours,
>   It is only borrowed plumage.

(D.T. Suzuki, *An Introduction to Zen Buddhism*,
quoted in Roca and Johnson 1999)

The views of three first-year students

It might be interesting before reading further to compare your current views about the kinds of language knowledge you feel you need with those of some other students. Barbara, Katie and Lynne are first-year students on a three-year teacher training course. When these discussions took place they had only been in college for two or three weeks. I want to focus in particular on some of their thoughts about the teaching of reading.

Barbara

Barbara is 36 years old. She has two children aged ten and eight and has worked for four years in a playgroup. Her thinking about language has been influenced by this work, and especially by watching her elder son, Graham, learn to read. She shared lots of stories with Graham and felt that before he started school he was very enthusiastic about books. During his first year at school a lot of emphasis was placed by his teacher on phoneme/grapheme relationships – on what is sometimes referred to as 'decoding' procedures. This process seemed to him to be very slow and he began to lose some of his initial enthusiasm and even to turn away from books. Barbara therefore, at this stage in her thinking, would emphasise the importance in the early years of teachers sharing texts with children, to carry on the enjoyment they have already experienced at home, or if they have not been so fortunate, to introduce them to the pleasures of reading.

Katie

Katie is 23 years old. Before coming to college she completed A level courses in English literature and language and general studies and was then in full-time work. She has one son, Kim, aged three. She agrees with Barbara about the importance of instilling in children a love of books and reading. However, she makes a distinction between the roles of parents and teachers. She sees it as the responsibility of the teacher, from the early years on, to turn the child into an independent reader. This would mean the child learning how to decode, how to build the smallest units of language, graphemes, into words, and then words into sentences and so on. In the meantime, whilst this is happening, it is the job of the parents to share books with their children, keeping the love of reading alive until such time as they can read for themselves. She feels that it is the media which have influenced her in her thinking about reading.

Lynne

Lynne is 20 years old. She has no children and so far has had little or no regular contact with any. She came on to a teacher training course after studying A level courses in politics and communications and then working in publishing for two years. She too feels that she has been heavily influenced by the media in her current thinking about reading. In Lynne's view, little can be done to turn children into readers until they have been given the knowledge of how to read independently. Like Katie, it seems sensible to Lynne to start with the smallest units of language, the phonemes, or sounds, which have been converted to letters on the page, and to give the children decoding strategies in the early years.

These were quite brief conversations and the three students were concentrating mainly on 'how to help children to start reading'. I think there might have been similar differences in emphasis if I had asked them to consider what children need to do next, after those initial reading stages have been achieved. I am quite sure also that if writing had been the topic for discussion, a range of views would have emerged from their group. I would expect some of them at this early stage in their training to hold a 'bottom-up' view of writing. By this I mean that they would emphasise the importance of starting from the smallest units of language, teaching children to make the letter shapes. This parallels the idea of starting to read by decoding the marks on the page, the letters of the alphabet in their various combinations. Other people would feel that it was important to ask children, from the very beginning, to write texts of all kinds, even though the texts might be indecipherable until the children had learned the rudiments of making the letters and combining them into words. Where do you stand at present on these issues?

The great literacy debate: conflicting views

Throughout my years in teacher training, my experience has been that more prospective teachers start their courses by holding a 'bottom-up' view than a 'top-down' one. The media are to some extent responsible for this, as Katie and Lynne both mentioned. In recent years, articles in the press have vilified what they call 'trendy, modern approaches' to the teaching of reading and have hailed a perceived return to phonics with enthusiasm. I think there is more to it than media pressure, however. I have the feeling that, viewed from many an adult's perspective, at least as far as Key Stage 1 children are concerned, to start from the smallest units seems extremely logical. How can children read until they know what the letters 'say'? How can they write until they can form the shapes of the letters?[1]

Does the starting point really matter?

Does it really matter, you may be wondering, whether we believe in starting from a text, or whether we believe in building up children's language knowledge from an emphasis on decoding words and learning spelling patterns, going on to rules for combining words into sentences and so on? I think it does. One of the difficulties about language knowledge is that there is just so much of it. And every primary teacher is aware of very many demands on the time available for study and preparation, let alone the time available for teaching. With the best will in the world, a generalist class teacher is going to struggle to find time to fit everything in. A natural reaction is to look for ways through this maze of information, for something to make life simpler. The lists of learning objectives in the National Literacy Strategy are seductive because they appear to give strong direction:

> It's got similes down for Year 4, Term 2, so here's my lesson on 'What is a simile?' After I've done that, I'll look around for a text that has some similes in it to help the class 'locate use of simile'.

Avoiding 'decontextualised' English activities

If we simply scour the text for similes, the question we must ask ourselves is 'Will it be of any benefit to Year 4 to know what a simile is?' Judith Atkinson (1995, p.49) suggests that the emphasis on presenting language 'information' to pupils is intentional in recent government documents:

Various national curriculum documents show that ... politicians have created a climate in which the key to the raising of standards is seen to be through the content rather than the processes of learning. In this context, English is a misfit and the documents have striven to give 'rigour' to the subject by stressing knowledge of and about literature. Pupils who know the difference between similes and metaphors ... have clearly learnt something: They also have knowledge which can be readily tested.

To be fair to whoever compiled the list of objectives in the National Literacy Strategy, the full text of the objective I referred to just now for Year 4, Term 2 reads: 'to understand the use of figurative language in poetry and prose; compare poetic phrasing with narrative/descriptive examples; locate use of simile.'

Putting language knowledge into context

The problem, especially for any primary teacher who is not an English specialist, is that it is much more straightforward to focus on the final part, to tell the class what a simile is, and then to play 'hunt the simile' in a text. However, the children are unlikely to benefit from this activity unless their teacher can accomplish the other two much more difficult parts of the objective: to help them to put poetic phrasing into some kind of context, and to understand why writers might choose to employ figurative language. We are then helping children with their own reading and writing by helping them to explore the difference similes will make to the range of meanings a writer is able to offer. For the non-specialist teacher (and for Year 4 too!) this is a tall order, though more worthwhile than mere simile-hunting.[2]

Language systems must support language processes!

Teachers who amass disparate bits of knowledge, such as what a simile is or what a pronoun is or, for that matter, what an autobiography is or what constitutes a title page, will not benefit their pupils thereby unless they can help them to build this information into coherent and ever-more detailed and sophisticated approaches to speaking, reading and writing. Perhaps the most fundamental aspect of language knowledge therefore for primary teachers to acquire is how to make language knowledge at each level – text, sentence and word – inform understanding at the other levels. They must know how to work from the top levels of the system down, *and* from the bottom, from the smallest units, up.

Reconciling opposing viewpoints

There is nothing new about multistrategy approaches to speaking, reading and writing. You may have met teachers who have been practising them successfully for many years. The National Curriculum makes it clear that this is the correct approach. In this extract from the programme of study for reading at Key Stage 1 (p.46), top-down *and* bottom-up reading cues are listed:

> Within a balanced and coherent programme, pupils should be taught to use the following knowledge, understanding and skills:
>
> - phonemic awareness and phonic knowledge
> - word recognition and graphic knowledge
>
> These two talk about learning the smallest bits of language, words and sounds and so are 'bottom up'.
>
> - grammatical awareness
> - contextual understanding
>
> These two refer to picking up cues from sentences and whole texts and so are 'top down'.

If we turn to the programmes of study for writing at Key Stage 1 (p.48), we read that pupils should be taught

- to assemble and develop ideas on paper and on screen
- to write extended texts with support.

At the same time as they are doing this,

- they should be taught to use capital letters, full stops, question marks and to begin to use commas
- they should be taught to write each letter of the alphabet
- they should be taught to spell common words.

I suspect that there are still some die-hard exclusively 'top-downers' and 'bottom-uppers' about, but if so, it is high time for them to each forsake their respective corners and meet in the middle of the ring. I have made plain my own feeling that the 'top' level, the text level, is the place to start almost all language study. However, we need to go much further than we have sometimes done in the past to help children to understand how texts, both written and spoken, are constructed and the significance of the syntactic and lexical choices speakers and writers have available to them to help them put their messages across.

Good classroom practice

You will see that I find it impossible to separate thoughts about language knowledge for primary teachers from considering the ways in which such knowledge will be presented to children in the primary classroom. To separate them might be to allow my readers to fall into the very trap I am urging all teachers to avoid, of acquiring decontextualised language information which is quickly forgotten or meaningless to the learner.[3] I know, because I have been a victim of this trap very recently. I saw the draft versions of the ITT National Curriculum and allowed myself to be panicked into planning some very decontextualised grammar sessions. I learned my lesson when one of my students observed at the end of one of these: 'I now know what a finite verb is, but I have nowhere to put it in my head.' I very much hope that no readers who persevere to the end of the book will find themselves in this position.

Using this book

The National Literacy Strategy makes clear the importance in the classroom of relating work at each language level to all the others. Chapters 9 and 10 explore these relationships with reference to four fiction and poetry texts and four non-fiction texts. For readers who are struggling to come to terms with the kinds of language knowledge encompassed by each of these levels, I thought it might be helpful to write about texts, sentences and words separately. I have done this in Chapters 4, 5, 6, 7 and 8. However, before starting this more detailed exploration of aspects of the language system, I want to look briefly at the significance for my language framework of what children have learned about language before they come to school.

Chapter 3

Building on preschool children's language knowledge

For me, one of the more regrettable themes to have run through most of my teaching career is the myth of the 'children who have no language'. The origins of this belief are too complex to trace in detail here, though readers who would like to explore its historical antecedents can find further reading in the notes for this chapter.[1] Often, the idea seems to have originated in a misreading of the work of Basil Bernstein. Almost always it was, indeed sometimes still is, children from families of low socioeconomic status who are labelled like this. I well remember, for example, standing in the entrance hall of a primary school on a large housing estate somewhere in south-west England, with the head teacher explaining to me that the children had no language, the reason being that they came from homes where there was no language. At that very moment, a meeting of the children's parents was taking place in the school hall a few feet away from where we were standing. The noise of conversation was deafening. As the head spoke, I looked pointedly in the direction of the din, but without eliciting any response. What is frequently meant, of course, when such judgements are made, is not that the children are literally dumb, but that they don't behave, linguistically, as the teachers would like them to. Language is acquired in a specific context. For most children this means first of all in their own homes, amongst parents and other caregivers. Sometimes children find the classroom a very different context for talk, and one which is not so supportive.

Language learning starts at home

All children, except for those with an exceptional degree of handicap, a gross defect of intelligence or a severe impairment of hearing, come to school having learned a great deal of language. This is true regardless of their social class. We can find evidence for this in Gordon Wells' (1987) 15-year longitudinal study of 128 children across the social spectrum in Bristol. Wells studied the tasks children can achieve through talk, such as:

- asking questions
- making plans
- recalling past events
- commenting on the world around them.

He also looked at the range of meanings they could make while carrying out those tasks, and the linguistic shape of their utterances. The findings of the research suggested that all the children, when recorded in their homes over a period extending from their first to their fifth birthdays, seemed to be learning in the same sort of way. By the end of this first phase of the research, for each child all the major linguistic systems were more or less in place. The children knew, for example,

- how to formulate questions in a variety of ways
- how to form past tenses
- how to phrase requests in a way that was likely to get a positive response.

Each child had a vocabulary of several thousand words. All this is miraculous enough in itself, if one considers that they were only just about five years old and had had few, if any, specific 'language lessons'. What is truly awesome is that some children at this age have already begun to operate in *more* than one language. Gordon Wells, who has a nice way with metaphors, describes this early feat of learning as 'a sheer climb up the face of a cliff' (p.32). It seems regrettable therefore that education research has repeatedly drawn attention to the language failings of some children. We do need to remind ourselves constantly of how much they have in fact achieved.

How do children learn to talk?

Researchers (psycholinguists this time and not educationalists), over the last 40 years at least, have approached this question from a variety of angles, leading to some quite famous 'fallings out' between them. You can find references to some of this work in the notes.[2] I will try in this chapter to focus on those aspects which have a particular bearing on the job of primary teachers, especially in Key Stage 1, as they strive to build on what has already been achieved by the children so far.

Chomsky: the Language Acquisition Device (LAD)

It is possible to see language learning as innate, part of a child's genetically transmitted inheritance, like walking upright or using the hands as tools. It was Chomsky who emphasised this approach. He suggested that inside the brain of each one of us is something called a Language Acquisition Device, or LAD for short, which predisposes us to learn and to use language. This is important to bear in mind if you have been inclined to take the view that children learn to speak by imitating adults. Of course, they do learn from the adults around them, but there is more to language learning than this. This is most obviously true when children say things that they have never heard an adult say. Examples might be:

- I runned all the way to school today.
- There are some sheeps in the school field.

These children have learned the general rule for forming the past tense, or for turning singular nouns into plural ones, and they are overapplying it to irregular examples. No budgerigar or parrot, learning by imitation only, would ever do this. Children appear to seek for the underlying principles that will account for the patterns they recognise in their language experiences. Adults, in their interactions with children, continually offer them new evidence of how things are done, and the children incorporate that evidence into their own developing language systems. They then use their systems to interact with the adults, they make errors, saying things the adult does not recognise as part of the 'mature' system, and then new evidence is given to the children which enables them to modify their original hypotheses. So one could say that in the first few years of life children are progressively reconstructing the language of their communities, on the basis of evidence from the more mature members of them. Wells (1987) quotes Andrew Locke in calling this 'the guided reinvention of language' (p.51).

Vygotsky and Bruner: social aspects of language learning

Vygotsky and Bruner, outstanding among many other researchers, have emphasised that adults and older children have a vital role to play at all stages in the development of babies' language. Chomsky himself stressed that it is the experience of being in a language-using environment that *triggers* the innate 'languaging mechanisms' in children. But even a stimulating environment is not enough. The image of children as being like plants, put into fertile soil and provided with an encouraging climate and then left to grow as and how they will, has, I think, been harmful to some children's progress, and has possibly prevented many from reaching their full potential. Many so-called 'privileged' children have their own spaces to play in, and are provided with televisions, computers, video games and so on. Yet in terms of their language development these things are not necessarily of very much help to them. What young children need is first-hand language experience: as much interaction as they can get, with adults and with older children, one-to-one or in small groups, engaging in topics of shared interest and encouraging an ever-extending range of purposes for talk.

The role of adults in language learning

Wells' research suggested that the quantity of language experienced by preschool children is a crucial factor: there is a clear relation between the children's rate of progress and the amount of language they experience with their parents and other adults. All the children Wells studied made progress, but those who experienced less conversation progressed at a slower rate. Another of Wells' findings in this area should give teachers food for thought, especially those in nursery and reception classes. He concluded that to be most helpful to children, their experience of conversation should be in one-to-one situations, with the adults talking about matters of interest and concern to the children. Both adults and children should be paying attention to the same objects or events. In the home, it is frequently the children who initiate the conversations, and supportive adults do their best to interpret situations in ways indicated by the children, though this is often difficult, even if the adult is very familiar with the child's ways of thinking and talking. It is vitally important to try to build shared structures of meaning. The advent of the literacy hour in England is making it more and more difficult for teachers to provide one-to-one interaction. There is already evidence to suggest that some Reception teachers themselves feel that the literacy hour format is inappropriate for the lower end of Key Stage 1 because the interaction with the children is mainly in whole-class or group situations.

The earliest stages of language learning

Preschool children, though they can cope well with conversation, given the kinds of supportive adults described above frequently do not have the conversational sophistication to deal with talking to people outside their social circle. They have acquired their language knowledge in very specific contexts, in daily, repeated activities such as washing and dressing, eating and going for walks to the shops and to other familiar places. They are particularly fortunate if these daily contexts have included adults singing songs and reciting nursery rhymes with them, sharing books, especially stories, or playing pretend games, such as sailing away on the sofa to a treasure island, stiff with pirates.

Babblings

Halliday (1973) has pointed out that when children first begin to 'talk' about things, and they do this, in a sense, even in the first few weeks of life, they use a language which bears no resemblance to that of any adult. You may think it odd to use the word 'language' about these early babblings at all. Yet children at this stage are indeed acquiring control over their 'sound-making apparatus', though it is true that all babies make more or less the same range of sounds, regardless of their nationality. Adults then, in one of their very first interventionist roles, come along and reinforce the sounds they recognise as being parts of their own 'phonemic set'. At first, babies have no sense of language as being for communicating with others, but the more this significant role for language becomes apparent, the more they want to share sounds with those around them. This is a vital stage in children's development as meaning makers and sharers. From this point on, they begin to have an inkling of how language can serve these purposes.

The sounds which are encouraged and repeated by the adults in a child's world are maintained and become ever-more systematised and organised, and the others die away. Of course, the sounds which adults reinforce are those that they recognise as the sounds of the language or languages they speak themselves, English or Welsh for example. 'Phoneme' is the technical term for one of these sounds. In English, there are approximately 44 such sounds. The number is approximate because the sounds speakers use vary slightly depending on their accent.

Once they have reached this stage, children have a 'two-tier' language system. They can make meanings, sometimes decipherable by those who know them well and share their lives. And they do this by building up a system of sounds, or phonemes, which becomes ever-more closely related to the sound system that those around them are using. The adults are very keen indeed to get at the meanings their children are trying to make, and will frequently ascribe meaning to a child's utterance based on their adult understanding. The whole process is 'meaning-driven'. The meanings are not just related to obtaining sustenance, though this must be very important to babies. Halliday identified at least five other purposes for 'speaking' in a one-year-old child he studied. These include:

- language for creating imaginary happenings
- language for finding things out
- language for joining in a range of collaborative activities with the adults and others around them.

The informative function of language

It is interesting to note that Halliday found that one function came quite a while after the others, at 22 months – interesting because this is the function which dominates adults' thinking about language and use of language. This is the informative, or 'I've got something to tell you' function. Halliday feels that the idea that language can be used as a means of communicating information to someone who does not already possess that information is a very sophisticated one. It depends on the internalisation of a complex set of linguistic concepts that young children do not possess. It's the only function which depends entirely on an exchange of words. It is often hard for even the most supportive adult to be sure what a child wants to tell them, sometimes as late as four or five years old.

Increasing vocabulary and syntax

With ever-greater, though frequently not total, control of the sound system within their reach, children can go on, with adult encouragement, to build a vocabulary of several thousand words before they are five years old. And slowly they gain control of the last tier of the adult 'languaging system'. This is the ability to combine words, using the rules of syntax, so that they can make meanings in ever more flexible ways. Semantics (knowledge of how to make meanings), sounds, words and syntax are now all in place.

Early language learning: its significance for primary teachers

There are a number of points about these learning processes which are important for primary teachers. Most important of all is the emphasis given by researchers such as Halliday and Wells to children as active meaning makers, originally indeed creating their own systems for making meaning without any thought as to whether they are understood or not. The concept of language as a shared social system, outside themselves as it were, and waiting to be acquired by them, only becomes a focus of their attention by gradual stages. Not all children will learn the shared system at the same rate, although most will have learned the fundamentals before starting school. I am concerned that the increased emphasis on teaching aspects of the language system, even at the lower end of Key Stage 1, will put unhelpful pressure on children who are still working their way towards full use of it, though they are by no means inarticulate children. Society expects teachers to help children to learn this system at all four levels – semantics, syntax, vocabulary and sounds. I hope by now, however, you will understand why I have continued to emphasise meaning making and sharing as the best language starting point in school, with the learning of syntax and vocabulary serving the ends of the meaning making and not the other way round. Otherwise, we are asking our four- and five-year-olds to do a complete about turn in their encounters with language. Margaret Donaldson's book *Children's Minds* (1978), though now some 21 years old, is well worth reading for its exploration of these issues.

Learning the language system: contrasting parental attitudes

The National Literacy Strategy has imposed the additional demand, from the Reception class on, of requiring children to have a metalanguage, a language for talking about language. It makes a lot of sense to be able to discuss aspects of the language system, once we are sure that children are ready for this. To be able to talk *about* language helps children to see it as an artefact, as something external to themselves, which can be thought about independently of using it to accomplish particular purposes in particular contexts. David Olson (1984) has made the point that some children have been prepared by their parents for this way of thinking by the manner in which the parents have supported their children's language acquisition. Parents whose own lives involve a lot of reading and writing are more likely to share the emphasis that we saw in some members of the case study group we looked at in Chapter 1. They are more likely to be aware of language as a socially constructed system, external to the individual child, and which he or she must therefore be inducted into. They may therefore set about teaching their children this system by breaking it down into different sized chunks, such as words and sentences, and then 'putting these under the microscope'. They are likely to believe that language can be *taught* to children. Other parents seem to adopt an approach closer to the image of the child as 'a plant in a well-manured garden', which I referred to earlier. Shirley Brice-Heath (1983) who has done interesting research into these contrasting parental attitudes, characterises these parents' views as 'No use me telling him – he just gotta learn'. Bruner (1983) points out that some parents introduce books to their children with the idea of using them as a way of teaching the children to talk. In other words, the parents are keen to extend their children's vocabulary, especially as regards the words for the names of objects or 'nouns'. In a fascinating article, Olson (1984) describes a mother who has taken the 'naming' game a stage further. Pointing to a frog jumping into a pond, the mother said, 'See! Jumping!' It's usually nouns, not verbs, or words for actions, that are the object of the naming game. Olson feels that this woman was not merely describing an event, but teaching the verb 'to jump', which, as he points out, is a very abstract concept. It's unusual for children to experience such a degree of explicit language teaching in their homes. It may well be counterproductive for parents to teach aspects of the language system too early: the end result might be to discourage their children's attempts to get to grips with it themselves.

Learning the language system: classroom approaches

Teachers as well as parents need to be very careful that children are not parroting bits of learning which are in fact quite meaningless to them. I was reminded of Olson's concern about promoting concepts which are too abstract for young children when watching one of the DfEE's literacy training videos. A Reception class are sharing 'The Jigaree' with their teacher, and a child is asked the name of the letter which starts the word 'Jigaree'. 'Jade,' he replies, perhaps drawing on his knowledge of the names of children in the school. The task for the primary teacher is to be sensitive to those children who have reached the stage where they can see the language as a system, those who are coming up to this, and those who as yet cannot distance themselves from the job of work the language is doing for them.

This is admittedly a tall order for a teacher in a busy class of some 30 children – not only to recognise these various stages but to provide differentiated support for each group. You can at least resolve to look for significant signs of progress. You should be on the lookout for example, if you plan to teach in nursery or

Reception classes, for children who use words to refer to mental processes. By this I mean words and phrases such as 'I wonder what ...', 'I think I know what ...', 'Let's pretend ... '. When you are sharing stories with children, you may find that only some of them can point out that a character in a story 'said X, but really he meant Y'. Children who can do these things have come to some objective understanding of language as a means of intending, thinking, knowing, planning, pretending, remembering, doubting, lying even. And they know too that these activities can be talked about. They will vary in the speed at which they arrive at these realisations, but until they have, the kind of self-conscious teaching of literacy which is included in the National Literacy Strategy for Reception classes is largely a waste of time.

Language learning takes time!

Where perhaps teachers of my generation have gone wrong is in forgetting that we *were* sensitive to the best kinds of language learning I have described in this chapter, but we talked about them as 'a starting point'. Yet I have seldom, if ever, been on an in-service course which was entitled 'Language Development: Phase Two', let alone 'Phase Three' or 'Four'. Occasionally, I have attended courses on so-called 'advanced reading skills' which turned out to be not about skills used by advanced readers. What has been described in this chapter *is* only a beginning, though a very impressive one, and one that may take some children quite a while to complete. The sophistications of text, syntax and vocabulary choices which the English language makes available are still to be discovered by five-year-olds who have at least 11 years of compulsory schooling ahead of them. We have possibly not done enough in the past to ensure that all children explore the possibilities the language offers, especially in their writing, but also in their reading and speaking. The rest of this book will be concerned with exploring some of the intricacies of this fascinating system, at each of these three levels, starting with text.

Chapter 4

Some characteristics of texts

What exactly is a text? I have used the term several times already in previous chapters, and if you are a mature entrant to teacher training – and possibly even if you are not – it may not be a term that you remember from your school days. The word 'text' in this book is being used to refer to complete and coherent passages of spoken or written language which come about because people live in social groups or communities and language is essential to them in living their lives.[1] Each time someone, or a group of people, sets out with the intention of carrying out a job of work which involves making or sharing verbal meaning in some way, they are creating a text. They might include:

- writing a report on a visit
- describing how to make a pancake
- gossiping with friends about the day's events.

Texts fulfil our purposes by allowing us to explore and express aspects of meaning in subjects we are concerned with or interested in. Sometimes, the making of the text is an end itself: we create it for the pleasure of the making and sharing. This probably applies to most stories and poems, or to the gossip I mentioned just now. Sometimes reading or writing a text is a means to something else – getting a new job, or having pancakes for dinner. Texts are produced with audiences or readers in mind, though, as for example in the case of a private diary, these readers may be the creators of the texts themselves. We shall see later that the image we have of the people who are to receive our texts exerts some influence on the ways in which we go about constructing the meaning in them.

'Text' is a useful term because it embraces all those many and varied ways of encapsulating meaning, formal and informal, that can be readily observed in use in every aspect of late twentieth-century society. 'Written texts' are of course not synonymous with 'books'. A book may contain within it several different types of text. Written texts can take the form of road signs or bus tickets or seed packets or chocolate bar wrappers. Frequently, diagrams, photographs, drawings and so on form an important part of how the meaning is created in these texts. It is important to develop the interest that even very young children show in environmental print, a generic term for all the kinds of written texts encountered in their homes and neighbourhoods. Children's first questions will probably be about what the text is for, but they will quickly go on to develop an interest in how the text is constructed. I was quickly put right, for example, when I once stated that my local supermarket was labelled 'Sainsbury's'. Examples like these should indicate to us that we need have no fear of discussing the choices of vocabulary and syntax that speakers and writers make when constructing a text, even with very young children. Once the children's interest has been engaged by the subject matter, they can very willingly be engaged in discussing text structure.

Texts can be written or spoken. These days, those are not the clear-cut distinctions they once were, although writers and speakers still find themselves contending with contrasting contexts and conditions in putting their texts together. As well as taking part in face-to-face interactions, most of us now use the telephone regularly, creating a different kind of spoken text. When we are e-mailing each other, are we drawing on our knowledge of how to participate in a speech event, or are we constructing a piece of writing? Our words will certainly appear, not on a piece of paper but on a screen, as will much else of what we read these days. Scrolling skills are now as much a part of reading texts as knowing where to start reading on the printed page. The amount of care we take in composing the e-mail will largely depend on its purpose and on our relations with the participant.

The differences between spoken and written texts[2]

Spontaneous talk

In face-to-face talk situations, each speaker learns to make lightning reactions to what the other speakers are saying and to adjust his or her next utterance accordingly. Sometimes these adjustments are not so slick, and everyone talks at once, or people interrupt each other. Sometimes there are brief silences. If you ever have the opportunity to make a study of spontaneous conversation, one of the interesting things you might observe is how long a group of people who are engaged in constructing a spoken text together – for example, a friendly chat in the college bar – can tolerate silence. It's also interesting to note who takes on the task of 'filling the gap'. In some talk situations such as a college lecture or an interview in a police station, the task of making sure that the discussion moves along is allocated to an individual person, by virtue of their role, though he or she may decide to pass the responsibility on to someone else. Primary children, at least once they are past Reception, have relatively few opportunities to introduce a topic for discussion in a classroom. They are usually put in the position of responding to a teacher's comments or questions, though in Wells' research, they were frequently observed to ask a question or start a conversation at home.

Talk which is rehearsed

There are spoken texts such as monologues and sermons which are constructed by one speaker. Many but by no means all of these are likely to have been planned to a greater or less extent before being delivered. Some may have been rehearsed. This planning is likely to result in the text having more of the characteristics of writing in its syntax and vocabulary. Indeed in some cases, faced, say, with the prospect of giving a talk to a very large, unknown audience, many of us would perhaps write down what we wanted to say, though even then, as we warmed to the task of delivering the speech, we might depart from the script and improvise a little from time to time.

Spontaneous writing

Of course, it would be a mistake to assume that just because a text is a written one it will have been carefully planned. Some writing is practically as spontaneous as some speech: A note pinned to the fridge door saying 'Gone to meating: back at 8', does not tax our powers of composition very much. Even if we feel a touch of uncertainty about the spelling of the third word, we are extremely unlikely to make ourselves late for the meeting by stopping to get out the dictionary. It really doesn't matter: our nearest and dearest will either not notice, or if they do, will hopefully put the mistake down to haste or a stressful day.

Writing which is planned and drafted

On very many occasions writers will go to great lengths to strive for correctness in written texts, not only in spelling, grammar and punctuation, but also in the construction of the text itself. We may try to look at some other texts, similar to the ones we are trying to create. We may ask someone to read through a text before submitting it to its intended audience. Does it 'sound right'? The interesting question then arises: how does the person we consult know whether it sounds right or not? How, for that matter, do we know how to participate in that conversation in the college bar without putting people's backs up or becoming a social misfit?

How do we learn what we know about text creation?

The answers to this question take us back to the learning processes undertaken by babies and young children which I described in Chapter 3. In that chapter, I referred to a crucial moment in all babies' language development when they become aware that the language they have been evolving for themselves can, if they make some adjustments to it, be used to share meanings with those around them. They have discovered, in other ways, that language is a social system. The adults and older children around them do all they can to introduce them to aspects of the system they use themselves. Young children are helped in very special ways:

- aspects of the system, such as sentence length, may be simplified
- significant words, especially nouns, are isolated
- these words are spoken in a very clear tone directed specifically to the children while the objects referred to are present
- sometimes explicit language 'lessons' are provided by some parents.

I was keen to emphasise in that chapter that the young children themselves take a lot of responsibility for their own learning. As they participate in creating spoken texts with those around them they take the data that the more experienced speakers offer to them and experiment with it, receiving feedback to help them to correct their mistakes. In this way they bring all aspects of their language ever closer to the ways in which the people around them are using language. To a very large extent, this is how we go on learning to create texts, though the contexts for learning change in crucial ways as we get older.

Control over text creation

I have described already in Chapter 3 how tolerance of mistakes decreases, even while children are still very young and inexperienced 'text creators'. Models of how things should be done and feedback on mistakes may not always be so readily available, or be offered in a friendly fashion. In his or her own classroom for example, the teacher almost always assumes the right to define what forms of spoken text are appropriate for the day-to-day management of affairs. Woe betide the child who uses the wrong form of text structure when asking to go to the toilet. To use words deemed 'rude' by a teacher, though they may be taken for granted in a child's home, can lead to some very hostile aspersions being cast on the child in question. It is assumed that we have learned certain 'language ways of the world' by the age of five, more by seven, more still by eleven. These are the ages at which primary children's language will be tested nationally – I listed in Chapter 1 some of the language achievements that are expected at these ages. The National Curriculum and the National Literacy Strategy make it very clear what spoken and written texts children should be able to produce at each of these stages and what kinds of texts they should be able to read.

How many different kinds of text are there?

Those mature entrants to teacher training I referred to earlier might remember the days when children in primary schools were expected to write their news and stories and, as they got older, to produce 'compositions'. In the 1960s, 'creative writing' was very much in vogue. As I remember it, this frequently involved writing free verse: in some cases, the form the text was to take was left to each child to decide. It would almost certainly turn out to be narrative of some kind. In 1978, an HMI report on *Primary Education in England* bemoaned the lack of range in the writing asked for by junior teachers.

During the 1960s and 1970s, teachers' perspective on writing, and on reading, was often a psychological rather than a sociological one. In many classrooms – mine was no exception – texts were frequently created by asking the children to employ one or more of their five senses, or in some cases to 'use their imagination' to produce a 'personal response' to a stimulus such as a piece of music, or a walk through the woods on a snowy morning. Where the language knowledge came from to enable these texts to be created was not so closely scrutinised. Clearly children acquired some knowledge from their reading, but as a great deal of emphasis was placed on originality, we did not want to see too much evidence of the reading material having been used as a model. Similarly, it was not considered to be a good idea to encourage children to act as writing response partners for each other in case one ended up with several pieces of very similar work.

The social origins of texts

Attitudes to text creation have now largely swung away from this emphasis on the isolated, soul-searching young writer. You can trace some of the influences on the changes in attitude in the notes to this chapter. In particular, I would like to draw attention to the important role of the National Writing Project in emphasising that classrooms can be seen as communities of writers and readers. This is important because it shifts the emphasis away from an individual search for personal meaning towards groups of people helping each other to define and refine what it is they want to say. The publications of that project helped teachers to become more aware of children having needs as writers very similar to those of any other writers in the world outside the classroom; need for time to plan and revise their work, to seek advice and positive comment on what they are producing and, perhaps most importantly, to look for models of how these writing tasks are carried out. The National Writing Project,[3] like the London University Writing Research before it,[4] also drew attention to the fact that the writing of certain types of texts, such as 'news' and stories, was overemphasised in schools, whilst other text types, and these frequently the ones that feature most prominently in the adult world, were almost entirely absent. The National Curriculum made it legally binding on all schools to ensure that children both read and write texts of many kinds, not just stories and poems. The vagueness of 'composition' disappeared and was replaced by specific lists of text types. Children were entitled to learn more about the variety of types of reading and writing (and, by now, speaking too) which their society values and finds interesting and worthwhile. Yet even in 1990, in a report entitled *English in the National Curriculum*, the Department of Education and Science was concerned that 'Narrative and descriptive writing in prose were almost universal. Although the older, abler children were capable of using writing to argue a case, to express opinions or to draw conclusions, most of them had little experience of those kinds of writing' (p.5). Presumably, the younger ones, and the less able, had none at all.

Genre theory[5]

I have referred to the lists of texts mentioned in the National Curriculum and in the National Literacy Strategy. The years between the publication of these two influential documents have seen the development of genre theory, originating first in Australian university departments, then disseminated in Australian schools, and now very influential in British schools. In the past, the word 'genre' has been used to group different types of literature: novels, short stories, poems for example. Novels as a group could be subdivided into more specific genres, such as detective novels, science fiction, historical novels. Poems fall into groups such as sonnets, ballads and lyrical poems. Even thus far, we can see some difficulties with the process. Where does the grouping stop? There are stories featuring male detectives and female detectives, blood-and-guts detective stories and more genteel ones of the Miss Marple variety. Couldn't some stories be put into more than one group? What purpose does the grouping serve? Are we to see these types and subtypes as offering rules, or if this is too strong a word, guidance, for the writing of these books? Does this create a set of expectations in readers? Can these expectations become in some sense binding?

New definitions of genre

If this seems complicated enough, the situation has been made even more complex in the last 20 years, during which the use of the term 'genre' has been extended. In the early 1980s, Frances Christie and her colleagues began to use the term to refer to any staged, purposeful cultural activity (Christie 1985). (By 'staged' they meant having a distinct schematic structure, with a similar beginning, middle and end.) Genres, they said, could be oral or written, and so could include sermons, recipes, letters, acceptance speeches and so on. At times, some genre theorists have given the impression that examples of any given genre shared an identical structure. This implies that an individual writer, wanting to produce his or her own specimen of a genre – a business letter say – must have internalised the rules of production for this type of text and must strictly adhere to them. Gunther Kress, in 1982, suggested that there is only a small number of genres in any written tradition, and perhaps even more surprisingly, that that number is fixed. However, ten years later, Kress had come to believe that 'generic form is never totally fixed, but is rather, always in process of change' (quoted in Dixon and Stratta 1999, unpub.). Beverley Derewianka, writing in 1996, defines a genre as a 'type of text used in a particular culture to achieve specific purposes' (p.7).

In describing a genre's characteristics she goes no further on this occasion than to say that each one has 'a number of characteristic elements which are organised *fairly* predictably' (p.8, my italics). There still seems to be a sense in which Derewianka and other writers such as Wray and Lewis (1997)[6] see genres as fixed in number. At least, this is what I infer from Derewianka's comment that 'there are of course many more genres than those described here' (p.11; she describes seven in this minibook). In a very similar comment, when offering guidance to teachers on how to help children construct six types of text, Wray and Lewis point out, 'There are of course many other kinds of non-fiction genres and many examples of mixed genre texts' (1997, p.118). I have to say that to me genre counting sometimes seems akin to the medieval obsession with discussing how many angels can dance on the point of a needle because, though writers are operating within a social context and are aware of social pressures and expectations, the human mind is inventive and very few text types will stay fixed for long.

Register

I have already referred in this chapter to the fact that when constructing a text writers or speakers may be affected by some features of their physical context, such as the surroundings, the temperature, the degree of comfort or discomfort they are feeling. For example, spontaneous face-to-face interaction calls for rapid decisions about what to say next. Many written texts on the other hand are produced in circumstances which provide opportunities for reflection and revision. Texts are written or spoken in moments of anguish, ecstasy, rage and so on. I have referred also to the effect on a composer of text of other people who are present, or who will eventually read the text. A story written for four-year-olds will look very different from one for adults. Text shape, layout, syntax and vocabulary are all different. Genre theorists use the concept of 'register' to describe these differences.[7] Stories, they claim, fulfil a cultural purpose which is, broadly speaking, to entertain. This makes them a genre: within this genre are a number of different 'registers' of story form.

Text creation: not a fixed process

As with genre counting, I feel some uneasiness about attempting to squeeze the richness of story forms into a specific number of registers. Perhaps it's unfair of me to choose as an example a genre where innovation is expected and encouraged and therefore where the number of text shapes proliferates. Would I feel differently about a type of writing less open to experimentation? Possibly. But we have to bear in mind that society is constantly changing in its needs, attitudes, expectations and values. Texts change, as do styles of dress, modes of transport, attitudes to eating meat, and so much else. So even a text type such as a recipe or a report must be seen as fluid and constantly evolving. At any one point in time, groups and individuals within a society vary in their willingness to tolerate innovation, or what they define as departures from the norm. If you fail to fill in a blank cheque along the lines laid down by your bank, it's unlikely that you will be given any money. At the other extreme, in many of the verbal arts, especially in poetry and song writing, or story writing, as I said just now, innovation is expected and is considered desirable. And there are many 'grey areas' in between. The kind of text I am writing now is perhaps one of them. You may be surprised to see sentences beginning with 'and'. You may feel irritated by my use of 'I' and 'you', or elided forms such as 'won't'. Perhaps you have been brought up to believe that these syntactic and vocabulary choices are more appropriate in spoken than in written texts. (It is possible of course that the publisher was irritated too and has edited out these features at a later stage in producing the book!)

The changing needs of society

Central to the view of language I am building in this book, is the image of the thinking, reflecting individual, located in a particular culture, at a particular time, and participating in reading, writing and speaking to others, at home, at work and in a variety of other social situations. Increasingly complex demands may be made on this person as he or she participates in creating texts or reading texts. We cannot know for certain what these demands will be in later life for today's five- to eleven-year-olds. However, as primary teachers, we can help them to cope by encouraging them to see texts as more than just, as Wray and Lewis (1997, p.105) put it 'transparent conveyers of meaning'. Texts are constructed in the way they are because speakers and writers, have made certain language choices. I must be honest and say that for me the concepts of genre and register, as Kress and others have explained them, seem to give too much emphasis to rules for text construction which are only apparent in a very broad sense when one looks at what people actually say and write. I am concerned that teachers may become more focused on teaching sets of 'rules for genre construction' than on helping children to find an appropriate voice for what it is they want to say. Like Dixon and Stratta, I find it more helpful to think of 'types of text', of no fixed number and sometimes with very fluid structural characteristics. These text types do have their origins in particular social occasions and fulfil particular social purposes and at a general level, when writers or speakers are engaged in similar tasks, there will be some degree of consistency in the language decisions they make. I suspect that the more confident people become in aspects of their 'language lives' the more some of them are prepared to experiment in their eagerness to get their meanings across, even with types of text that appear relatively fixed.

   Primary teachers on the other hand are frequently dealing with the least confident, because the youngest and most socially inexperienced, members of society. There is no doubt in my mind that in the past we have not done enough as teachers, first to give children experience of reading texts constructed in different ways, to help to bring to their notice what skilled and experienced writers and speakers have done and then to help the children to make use of the full range of language choices available to them. Government tests, especially of 11-year-olds, are revealing that it is in coping with a range of writing tasks, rather than in reading, that children are failing to reach the expected standards. I have given one reason already in this chapter for why this might be so: too much attention has traditionally been given to the writing of stories and news. I would like to return to story writing in a later part of the chapter, but I want to look first in a little more detail at some aspects of non-narrative texts.

Extending the range: issues in creating non-narrative texts

Successive politicians have been keen on urging teachers to 'get back to basics' when teaching children to write. They usually seem to mean by this showing the children how to punctuate a sentence or produce a more legible script. In fact, the most 'basic' problem a writer faces is what to write about, and then, once poised with pen in hand (or seated at the keyboard), how to begin to order one's ideas. The National Curriculum speaks of chronological ordering of ideas and 'non-chronological', as if these two labels were somehow of the same kind. To order one's ideas chronologically means to put things down more or less in the order in which they happened. This frequently, but by no means always, happens in stories: 'One day … suddenly … then … next …' 'Then' is one of the earliest connectives grasped by children and is much overused to handle what has come to be called 'bed-to-bed' writing (when the child describes what happens from getting up in the morning to going to bed at night). A lot of emphasis in primary schools has been placed, quite rightly, on learning from first-hand experience. Visits are made, for example, to the local Roman villa or the local supermarket. In many a classroom, seeds are planted or chickens are hatched. It is not just in narrative that children have frequent resort to chronological writing. The 'bed-to-bed' approach has been employed by children to write about learning experiences such as each of the above, though this may not at all have been the teacher's intention. How else could the tasks have been organised?

Choosing a structure

To speak of 'non-chronological' ordering is not very much help at first sight because it is an umbrella term which merely refers to any text where the points are not ordered in a time sequence. It is essential for teachers to have experience at first hand of the different ways in which texts can be ordered, so that they have a clear view of the possibilities available when they discuss a writing task with a child. Let us take a visit to a Roman villa as an example. It offers a wealth of writing opportunities which might be shared out around the class. Stories, poems and plays come readily to mind, but we are pursuing non-fiction possibilities here.

Defining a purpose

What might the teacher's learning objectives have been in organising the visit and what kinds of writing will support these learning objectives? Perhaps the domestic life of the Romano Britons was the major focus with the children being asked to prepare a wall display or a class book.

An explanatory text

Some children may want to write about how the villa was heated in winter. What is involved in carrying out this writing task successfully?

- The writer must provide an explanation of a process, not so that readers can carry it out themselves, but so that they understand how it was done.
- The points must be presented in a logical sequence, from showing how and where a source of heat is introduced into the villa to explaining how the heat is maintained and disseminated through the rooms.
- It is likely that the writer's task will be helped by the inclusion of drawings or diagrams.

A procedural text

Other children might have been asked to find out about the diet of the people who lived in the villa, and to do some research into styles of eating. They will produce a menu for a Roman banquet, with recipes for some of the dishes.

- They will need models for recipe writing.
- Some feedback would be useful on whether their instructions seem clear enough to produce an edible result.

It's likely that their readers would find it helpful, especially if they are actually going to try their hands at some cooking, to have items arranged in list form. Readers of recipes want to be told exactly what to do, especially when poised over a hot stove with hungry guests expecting to be fed.

A report

One of the more demanding writing tasks might be to write about 'What it was like to live in Roman Britain'. This is difficult for a number of reasons: it means scanning quite a lot of aspects of Roman life and then organising them into some sort of logical sequence. One possibility among several might be to have an introductory sentence, such as 'Life was quite pleasant for most people in Roman Britain, though there were some problems'. This would enable the writer to sort out some examples of things which were pleasant and write about them, and then provide some examples of problems.

Textual cohesion

It would be by no means easy to ensure a successful conclusion to all these writing tasks, even if we only think for the moment about potential problems at the text level, which are what I regard as the 'basic' ones. For one thing, readers expect texts to hang together, to appear to be 'all of a piece' unless there is some very good reason for their changing their shape part way through. The technical term for this is 'cohesion'. I want to discuss it here at the text level and shall have more to say about how writers can maintain cohesion at the sentence and word levels in subsequent chapters.

The explanatory text

If we are told that we are going to have an explanation of Roman central heating presented to us, we, as mature adult readers and writers, expect the piece to deal with sources of heat, with underground passages, types of tile and so on. Some of these things, rather than people, will turn out to be the subjects of the sentences. We expect these sentences to be presented to us as a series of general statements about how things were done over the period of the Roman occupation. This means that the piece will be in the past tense, but will not deal with any specific date or place. Our 'heating group' may start off well enough with a sentence about how the Romans heated their houses by using an under-floor system, but, given some uncertainty about the more technical details, might soon resort to a chronological account of what they saw. 'We went through some underground passages and then we noticed …' This can all too easily turn into full-blown narrative, with an account of how Gary tripped or Samantha got lost. The subjects of the sentences are now themselves, or their friends, and events are related sequentially. The text has lost its cohesion.

The procedural text

The recipe writers, though they may be familiar in a general way with the structure of a recipe, may fail to appreciate everything readers need to know in order to produce roast field mouse (though it's unlikely that the readers will be actually called upon to do so!). How much knowledge about basic cookery skills can be assumed in one's readers? Must they be told every single thing or can some stages in the process be left to their common sense? Judging what the reader can be assumed to know is an important part of any text construction. This applies both to what they might know about the subject and also about reading this type of text. (Think of a knitting pattern, for example.) Writers need to offer just the right number of cues to steer their readers along without either patronising them or baffling them to the point where they abandon the text.

The report text

The greatest danger is perhaps that those faced with writing a report on life in Roman Britain will resort to copying chunks from a reference book. The heating group have some first-hand experience they can refer to after their visit. They may have made notes or sketches. The recipe group have models to look at and will in all probability have seen recipes in newspapers at least. To talk about the quality of life in Britain at the time of the Romans means holding in your head quite a lot of specific examples about homes and clothes and occupations and a great deal else. All of this information has to be sifted and organised by means of some generalising statements: an example might be 'One very good thing about life at this time was the plumbing'. Then some flesh has to be put on these bare bones. Not only that, but disadvantages have to be weighed against advantages and some conclusion reached. Generally speaking, primary teachers should not expect children to be able to make successful generalising statements in non-fiction texts *except* where these are tightly rooted in some first-hand experience, though in this I would include experience gained in drama or role play situations. This last group, for example, might first have role played a group of villa dwellers and discussed what they found pleasant, and what irksome about their lives as they 'sat in the bath house'!

Problems of turning experience into words

There are three elements to juggle with in shaping aspects of an experience into a piece of writing: the subject, the writer and the reader. Sometimes it seems inappropriate for writers to be mentioned directly in their finished pieces. On other occasions it is perfectly acceptable for them to present information directly as they saw it, using the first person pronouns 'I' or 'we'. The latter text structure is easier to handle in many ways, especially if the subject is something one is still trying to get to grips with. As regards the readers of the texts, children are frequently in the position of writing texts for people (teachers) who know more about the subject than they do. This does not make it easy for them to decide how much to tell. It is much easier to write texts for people who are genuinely seeking for enlightenment or entertainment. Teachers can turn themselves into such readers at various stages in the writing process, and can also help children by making available other types of reader.

There are, of course, other levels of decision making that writers must face. Texts will consist of sentences or phrases and writers or speakers must decide how to structure those. Vocabulary too will need careful handling. I will return to these kinds of language choice in later chapters.

Helping children to make text level decisions

This is not a book about how to teach writing. However, I cannot resist urging teachers to allocate enough time to discussing with children what kind of text they feel would be appropriate on a given occasion. The long years of story writing, or of 'telling what we did', have left their mark on children and they assume – or their parents, who may be trying to help them, assume – that this is what the teacher wants. Again, if the children have had experience of writing mainly narratives, they may suppose, even when asked to search for information in text and to present it factually, that they are expected to invent some of their answer or to embellish the facts in some way. Decisions like this need to be agreed beforehand, or the text that is eventually presented may be unfairly criticised because it bears disappointingly little resemblance to what the teacher had in mind.

The most common forms of non-fiction text

One of the good things about the National Literacy Strategy is that it provides whole-class time for shared reading and discussion of text features, followed by shared writing, which is an opportunity for teachers to model the kinds of decision making I have outlined above.

Some of my readers, as I have acknowledged already, may feel far from confident at this particular point in their careers about their ability to discuss the significant features of a range of texts, particularly non-fiction texts, for 15 minutes several times a week. It may be of some comfort to you to know that researchers who have studied large numbers of texts, such as the Australian genre theorists I mentioned earlier, suggest that very large numbers of non-fiction texts are written to fulfil one or other of six purposes. Some texts provide *recounts* of events the speaker or writer has participated in or has heard about. They are frequently chronologically ordered, and, when children produce them, will sometimes describe everything from what the child had for breakfast to being sick in the coach on the way home (what I earlier called 'bed-to-bed' writing). A second large group is of the '*procedural*' type, which tells the reader how to do something – cook a roast field mouse, for example. '*Reports*' is a label which can be used for texts which deal with 'how things are' (or were, in Roman Britain, for example). They require the writer or speaker to deal in generalisations, though probably illustrated with specific examples of the particular phenomenon that is being discussed. A fourth group of non-fiction texts provides *explanations* of how or why something happens: in my example, how Roman central heating works. The last two frequently encountered purposes for producing non-fiction, which I did not include in my Roman Britain list, have been found to be texts *presenting an argument*, and texts *discussing an issue*. As an example of this last category, I might perhaps have included in my list a group of children writing a letter to a newspaper about the lack of amenities provided for tourists at the villa, though this would have taken me rather outside my target of a wall display or a class book.

Writing frames

When we set out to discuss an issue with a group of friends, the textual cohesion I spoke about above is not such an important matter. We expect the talk to range to and fro. We can back track easily, by inserting into the conversation something we meant to say earlier. As we talk, we are likely to think of more ideas, and to be prompted by the others to remember things we had forgotten. Someone may take on the role of chair and attempt to keep order, but on many occasions the talk will be a free-for-all, and may indeed become very *in*coherent. Constructing written texts can be a much more lonely business, and the demands to organise what we have to say can be much greater. One's gran may be so pleased to get a letter that she doesn't mind what order the points come in, but other readers will be less forgiving. The more formal and abstract the types of text to be constructed the greater the demand, especially on an inexperienced writer. Hence the value of the response partners I referred to in an earlier chapter and the importance of offering guidance in the whole text portion of the literacy hour. There will still be many occasions when a class may be faced with getting on with a piece of writing without immediate help being available. Wray and Lewis (1997) suggest offering some children an outline structure in the form of a writing frame to support them in the six most frequently occurring non-fiction written forms. The writing frame would suggest to children those stages in the construction of the text which I have already referred to, and might offer some starting phrases, or phrases for linking one stage of the text with the next: 'on the one hand …' or 'nevertheless …' or 'I would like to begin by …'. As they point out, there are many possible writing frames for each of the six broad purposes for writing, and it is important that any frame suggested to children stays flexible and does not become a rigid form. To my mind, a frame should also be regarded like a pair of water wings, with all the dangers of overdependence that they can produce, and every effort should be made to dispense with its use as quickly as possible. I have seen story frames used quite frequently, but, in fact, it is probably with the more complex structures of non-narrative texts that some children need help.

Chapter 5

Making sense of texts

A writer's or speaker's purpose in embarking on a text is almost always to make meaning of some kind or other. Occasionally, as when a child is crying in the middle of the night, it's not so much the meanings that are important as that someone is there, and making soothing noises. It needs to be remembered that the meanings we all strive to make are often far from straightforward. We can use language in order to tell lies, or to present a very biased view of events. In a spoken text, speakers will very often have instant feedback on how their meanings are being received, with comments like, 'I don't understand a word of that', or 'Come off it, who are you trying to kid', and so on. They can then try to take further steps, assuming they are allowed to say more. Writers are not often there to comment on their meanings, but can offer cues to their readers about how they expect or hope their texts to be read. However, just as a group of speakers are interacting with each other to make meaning, so readers will, in a sense, interact with the texts they are reading, and the meanings they take from those texts will depend on some of the factors I have mentioned already: their age, their knowledge of this subject, their experience of this kind of text, their opinion of the writer and so on. It would be a great mistake to think that 'comprehension', or understanding a text, consists of quarrying it for little chunks of meaning which the writer has built in to it. As we become used to reading a particular type of text we build up pleasurable anticipation of what we expect to find: we bring this knowledge and experience to bear in creating the meaning in our own minds, though of course it would be a very poor reader who deliberately ignored the cues the writer has provided. To be a good reader means to set up a dialogue with the text inside one's own head, with the words the writer has provided sparking off pictures, ideas, comparisons and so on.

Reading as an active process

This may be a view of reading that you have not thought about very much before, especially if you were unfortunate enough to have teachers who talked you through a text line by line, or even perhaps gave you dictated notes on its meaning. You may feel that you lack confidence in your ability to interact with the meanings of texts in this way. I hope that you will pursue this approach further, perhaps by using some of the notes provided for this chapter.[1] Whilst most adults, given perhaps some encouragement to read like this, can carry out that 'dialogue in the head' which I spoke about just now, when you come to the point where you are helping primary children to read like this you will need to plan for more active involvement with the texts. One of your most important tasks in teaching reading will be to think about ways of ensuring lively explorations of the meanings of texts with your class. You need to convince the children that it is not the teacher alone who has the key to unlock the meaning, that it's acceptable to disagree over what something means, provided the readers have considered the evidence in front of them.

A range of reading behaviours

There is another important point to bear in mind about describing reading as 'creating meaning in our own minds'. Not only will different readers obtain different meanings from a text, but the same reader, reading on different occasions, will find different meanings. Some texts, and many poems are a good example of this, have layers of meaning in them which only come to light after many readings, and after accruing a lot of experience in reading poetry. Of course, it's not always like this. The act of reading is not always concerned with pondering on meaning. No one wants to tease out the meaning of a railway timetable. To have to do so might result in missing the train, or arriving at the wrong destination. We want the writer to guide us, by means of columns, subheadings, large print, or whatever is most helpful, to the part of the text we need, and we will ignore the rest. But to tease out the meaning of a story or a poem is part of the pleasure of reading the text. On these occasions, we feel the language of the text, along the skin and in the imagination. We relish the relationship of one part of the text with another, like the movements in a symphony or as when gazing at a painting. We enjoy the feeling of never being really sure whether we have missed something, or whether the writer's cues could have been interpreted differently.

Complex purposes for reading

It is sometimes suggested that the reader goes to non-fiction in order to learn, rather than simply for enjoyment or 'to lose oneself in another world' which many see as the main reasons for reading fiction or poetry. These definitions are simplistic. It is possible to learn something about rivers from reading *The Wind in the Willows*, although this was not Kenneth Grahame's main reason for writing it. It is possible to read a biography (or a DIY manual if you are that way inclined) simply for enjoyment and to lose yourself in the text.

Approaches to the structuring of fiction and non-fiction texts

It is the case that there are some fundamental differences in the way fiction and non-fiction texts are constructed, though even here there are exceptions. A poem or a work of fiction has been conceived as a whole. It is usual to speak of story structure as comprising a beginning, a middle and an end. All texts, of course, inevitably have a beginning, middle and end – even notes to the milkman. What is implied here is that the writer of a story or a poem has paid very close attention to the relationship between the beginning, the middle and the end. To read them in any other order (though some people do insist on reading the end of a story first!) is to do damage to the author's intentions. The relationship between each part adds something to the meaning of the whole.

It is for this reason that it is unfair to a story writer or a poet to take a section of text and study it without also seeing it in its context. It is rather like looking at one water lily in a Monet painting while the rest of the painting is covered up. It is not a meaningless activity, but in trying to make meaning we are not receiving the data the creator of the piece intended us to. As we become more familiar with a writer's or a painter's work, we *can* appreciate a detail seen in isolation, because we have in our minds our knowledge of the rest of the text on which to draw. Primary-age children, even in Key Stage 2, are not usually in this position.

The relationship of the parts to the whole is not the same in a non-fiction text. Sometimes there is an expectation on the part of the writer that the reader will start at the beginning and read through to the end. Indeed, in a 'process' text such as 'How to Make a Chocolate Cake' it would be very foolish not to do so. Generally though, it is possible, if one is so inclined, to approach the text in a more piecemeal fashion, and indeed, the text itself should support readers in doing just that. Even in a biography, where the points are likely to be arranged in chronological order as they are in many a story, it may be that readers do not want to know about the person's early life, and will use the chapter headings to guide them to the part of the life that they are interested in. Chapters in turn may be subdivided with clear headings, enabling the reader to skim through, scanning the pages for a useful section.

There is an implication in what I have said about approaches to non-fiction texts that very often, though not always, readers approach them with a question or questions in mind to which they are seeking an answer or more information. They may be interested in the writer's views on an issue, as in a newspaper editorial, or they may want to make something or carry out a particular process. You may find it useful to remind yourself of the six most frequently found forms of non-fiction text which I listed in Chapter 4.

Having fun with meaning

Whatever the type of text, reading should be seen from the earliest stages in a reader's life as a search for meaning. This search can, of course, take all sorts of forms, some of them very lighthearted. Many young children enjoy nonsense texts more than anything, where the writer may appear to have turned meaning on its head. Recently, I was told about a class of ten-year-olds, all boys, who were asked at the end of the school year which language activities they had enjoyed the most. Two things were clear favourites. One was some work on alliteration which you may have tried yourselves. A letter of the alphabet is chosen and then, starting with 'one' then 'two' and 'three' etc., followed by their personal choice of words from lists provided in columns labelled

ADJECTIVE   NOUN   VERB   NOUN

the boys conjured up such amazing spectacles as: 'one winsome whale wondering whether to waltz' and 'two terrible twins twisting twenty twigs'. Another lesson the boys remembered with great enjoyment was when they read this poem.

I saw a Peacock with a fiery tail
I saw a blazing Comet drop down hail,
I saw a Cloud with ivy circled round,
I saw a sturdy Oak creep on the ground,
I saw a Pismire swallow up a whale,
I saw a raging Sea brim full of ale,
I saw a Venice Glass sixteen foot deep,
I saw a Well full of men's tears that weep,
I saw their Eyes all in a flame of fire,
I saw a House as big as the moon and higher,
I saw the Sun even in the midst of night,
I saw the Man that saw this wondrous sight.
Anon.

What the boys said they enjoyed about the experience was the nonsensical element of it – the house as big as the moon, the sun in the midst of night. Alternatively, some readers will enjoy creating meaning of a surreal kind, conjuring up in their minds vivid images like the peacock with the fiery tail, or the eyes in a flame of fire. Or the poem can be read in yet another way:

I saw a peacock.
With a fiery tail I saw a blazing comet.
Drop down hail I saw a Cloud.
With ivy circled round I saw a sturdy Oak.

Read like this, though the syntax is a bit peculiar, the poem makes literal sense and some readers will get pleasure from having 'broken the code'.

Meanings beyond the literal

Unlocking the meaning in stories and in poems frequently depends on considering the writer's use of figurative language. I shall say more about this in Chapter 7. Some readers struggle to get enjoyment from exploring the significance of metaphors and similes. All teachers collect memories of triumphs and disasters. One of the latter that sticks in my mind was of a boy who looked at me after my class had shared a poem about a river, sad because a man had drowned in its waters. 'Rivers,' he said to me, witheringly, 'don't talk'.

Uncovering layers of meaning

All primary teachers want to enlarge their pupils' reading repertoires. In recent years we have had the good sense to offer children a wider choice of texts and to encourage them to bring texts of their own choosing into the classroom. Readers, as I have pointed out already, will approach the same text differently at different times in their lives. The door labelled 'poetry' or 'fiction' is not necessarily going to slam shut for ever. It is very important to offer even young readers quality texts whose meanings can be unpeeled like the layers of an onion. It may take years to realise what layers were in the text, and yet I believe that some of that subtlety of meaning will be apparent even to a relatively inexperienced reader. Reading scheme books are excellent for developing reading strategies and skills, but very rarely do they offer these 'layers' which so richly reward continual rereading, pondering and discussion. Yet it must not be a case of 'practise on the scheme texts now and then later on you'll be able to tackle some more interesting ones'. Reading is a very difficult business and young readers must be convinced that the game is worth the candle. The texts we offer them, from the start, must be fun, wacky, engrossing, intriguing and scary, endlessly challenging our ways of looking at life.

Quality in fictional texts

What counts as quality in fiction texts is a matter of subjective judgement to some extent. I very much meant what I said in Chapter 1 about developing your own enthusiasms and tastes as readers. To develop tastes and preferences means also developing a feel for the way certain authors do things. I will risk offering at least an example here of what *I* mean by quality, what to me 'layers of meaning' might refer to, though one example doesn't make a definition! I want to talk about a picture book which features very frequently in discussions of children's literature, though I have no regrets about mentioning it yet again. It is *Where the Wild Things Are,* by Maurice Sendak (1963). The book opens with Max, the hero of the story, dressed in his wolf suit, and 'making mischief of one kind or another'. As a result, his mother called him 'WILD THING' and sent him to his room without any supper. The reader is shown, rather than told, some of the kinds of mischief he got up to. This has the advantage of instantly involving the reader in the 'onion peeling' kinds of reading I referred to earlier. We have choices as readers: we can go on to find out what happened next; we can become involved in thinking about our reactions to what Max did which annoyed his mother so much; or we might want to think or talk about how we feel about his punishment.

What happened next was certainly very interesting. 'That very night in Max's room a forest grew and grew until his ceiling was hung with vines and the walls became the world all around ...' There are rich opportunities here for reading between the lines. Some readers will bring previous experience to bear of escaping from reality into a world of their own creation. Some may be reminded of other texts that they have read like this one. On a first reading, many will not want to pause at all at this point, but will want to find out more about the story. The high point comes when Max arrived at the 'place where the wild things are', and we follow his progress in building a relationship with them. A literal reading enables us to react with a shiver of horror at their 'terrible roars', their 'terrible teeth' and their 'terrible claws'. Or readers might choose to find them funny, or even cuddly. Max was certainly not phased by them. He became their king and they recognised him as 'the most wild thing of all'. He was in charge, and was able to order them off to bed without any supper.

Just when he seemed all set for a life of endless 'wild rumpuses' we are told that 'from far away across the world he smelled good things to eat' and so decided to give up being king of where the wild things were. The wild things were not pleased and begged him to stay. They even threatened to eat him, but Max was not at all put out by their threats. He stepped into his private boat and sailed back into 'the night of his very own room', where he found his supper waiting for him. Some of the most interesting opportunities for exploring beneath the surface of the text come in discussing (or enacting) what life would have been like with the wild things. Could Max have gone on for ever? Why did he decide not to? It may take many readings, even many years, before children can explore all the links and layers which the book makes possible.

We can compare this text with one that seems similar in some ways, *Row Your Boat*, a rhyming text by Pippa Goodhart, with illustrations by Stephen Lambert (1997). Two children find themselves, like Max, sailing away in a boat, but here we are *told* rather than shown that 'life is but a dream', and so we have not really engaged the deeper levels of our own 'meaning-making apparatus' as readers when we arrive at the dream land the writer has created. It is difficult to read in any other way but literally about the elephants, monkeys, snakes and spiders who await the children's arrival. There is none of the delicious ambiguity of Sendak's creations. In his book we see Max befriending the creatures, even becoming their king, and yet, and yet ... they are still 'terrible', the writer reminds us, and do actually threaten to eat him. We as readers must decide how we are going to interpret this. In Pippa Goodhart's book, when the lion roars, there is no ambiguity at all. The children very wisely decide to run back to the boat

Before the lion catches us
And eats us for his tea!

There is nothing wrong with this text. It is delightful in many ways. The words are set to music and the children will very much enjoy singing them. It does not have the quality of Sendak's text in the sense that, in my opinion at least, it will not repay many rereadings, because most of its meaning resides on a literal level. It asks very much less of its readers.

In this chapter and the last I have given a fairly brief overview of some of the issues involved in writing and reading texts. In Chapters 8 and 9 I shall take some of these points further by looking at specific examples of fiction and non-fiction texts. Texts depend of course on arrangements of words to create their effects, and it is to the variety of ways of arranging them that I shall turn next.

Chapter 6

What big teeth you have, grammar!

I chose this title for Chapter 6 because many people seem to be afraid of grammar, seeing it as a set of rules waiting to catch them out. I want to persuade you that grammar should rather be seen as a resource, serving writers' and speakers' purposes as they struggle to express meanings in the texts they are creating. The next two chapters will not turn you into an expert on English grammar, but I hope that they will at least begin to make clear what a knowledge of grammar has to offer to primary teachers, and therefore to the children in their classes. In the chapter notes I have listed some useful books to help you to build on the information here.[1]

Section 1: What is grammar?

It is possible, but fairly unusual to find texts which consist of one or two words only. There are examples, spoken or written, such as:

• Help!
• Nice day!
• No entry.

These sentences, known as minor sentences, don't obey the usual rules of text construction. For more information on minor sentences, see Crystal (1988). Lists are another example of texts which can consist of words in groups or in isolation: perhaps one reason why they are a popular text type among young writers is because the writer is free from the constraints of the rules of syntax.

Syntax

'Syntax' is the term used for the set of rules governing the ways in which words are regularly combined into clauses appropriate for a particular text, including rules for word order and word endings (inflections). It is possible to invent a sentence which obeys the rules of syntax, but is perfectly meaningless, as in

- Siv grockles lubed transomly.

Though you have never seen these words before, it is possible to deduce from the word order and endings such as 'ed' and 'ly' what work each of these words is doing, though you can have little or no idea of the semantics, or meaning, of the sentence. To understand a little more about semantic processing, or how we make meaning from what we hear or read, think about a sentence like

- Dogs must be carried on the underground.

Unless they can process the meaning of this correctly, all those who have left Fido at home will be heading for the bus stop.

Inflectional endings

The term 'inflection' refers to the ways in which words change their spellings , or acquire extra bits at the beginning or the end, depending on the work the words do in a sentence (for example, he runs, he is runn*ing*, he r*an*). The parts added on are known as prefixes if they are attached to the beginning of a root word, and suffixes if they are added on at the end.

How words work within sentences

Grammar also provides a description of how words can function in different ways in sentences, depending on their place in the sentence and their relationship with other words. For example, in the sentence, 'I grow beetroot in my allotment' the word *beetroot* is functioning as a noun, but in the sentence 'Beetroot sandwiches were Fred's favourites' *beetroot* is being used as an adjective, to describe 'sandwiches'. It might be possible to invent a sentence in which *beetroot* becomes a verb.

- 'What did you do for lunch today?'
  'Oh, today I beetrooted, and I shall courgette tomorrow.'

A fuller definition of these word classes – 'noun', 'verb' and 'adjective' – can be found later in this chapter.

Is it really necessary to teach grammar?

It's clear that the study of grammar so totally disappeared from the curricula of some schools that many people have been left with a feeling of complete ignorance about it. Now, the National Literacy Strategy and the National Curriculum for ITT are demanding that primary teachers have fairly detailed knowledge. One of the most difficult questions to give a clear answer to, though I am sure you are hoping for one, is 'Is it necessary to provide children with specific grammar teaching?' Many times recently I have heard people say 'I've lived for 30 [or 40 or 50] years without knowing what a preposition was, and it hasn't done me any harm! Why do I have to teach it to children?' One of the most difficult but most important tasks for primary teachers is to ensure that they pass on knowledge of grammar to children in such a way that it helps to make the children more discriminating readers, writers and speakers and empowers them to produce written and spoken texts which both embody what it is they want to say and make a suitable impact on those listening or reading.

What does it mean to be knowledgeable about grammar?

Just because some people can't state explicitly what a preposition is certainly does not mean that they are unable to express themselves adequately in speech or in writing. One of the most important distinctions to be clear about as you acquire more knowledge about language is the difference between implicit and explicit language knowledge. I have described in previous chapters how we learn the processes involved in putting language together, as people who are actively participating in carrying a range of language jobs or functions in a society. I have spoken of the kinds of feedback we all receive which enable us to fine tune our utterances so that we accomplish our purposes and satisfy the needs of those we are communicating with. When some people express an ignorance or fear of the rules of grammar, they may mean that they cannot put these rules into words, can't explain what a conjunction is, or identify a subordinate clause in a sentence, though their speech and writing will be full of prepositions, conjunctions and subordinate clauses.

Finding the right context for grammar teaching

If you are one of those who have doubts about the value of grammar teaching, I think it is certainly worth considering whether a certain amount of grammatical knowledge, provided it is taught in context, supports and extends children's implicit use of language. This may be especially true for those children I referred to in an earlier chapter who do not pick up a variety of sentence patterns simply from being exposed to them as readers and speakers, but who might be able to bring more variety to the texts they create, and more sensitivity to other writers' and speakers' achievements, if they had more explicit teaching.

Section 2: Standard English and regional varieties

There are almost certainly some people whose dislike of grammar is connected with a sense of inadequacy about their powers as language users. One of my earliest memories is of people coming to our house in a small northern mill town to ask my mother or father to help them to put a formal letter together or to make an 'official' telephone call for them. One might have hoped that many years since then of free state education would have eradicated people's feelings of inadequacy, but this seems to be not entirely the case. We have probably all seen those advertisements in newspapers, with the headline 'Why Are You Shamed By Your Mistakes In English?' They have been appearing for many years now, so presumably the people who market the Practical English Programme, as it is called, are tapping into a large well of insecure language users. The latest example of the advertisements that I have seen occurred in a national broadsheet newspaper the day before I started to write this chapter. The organisers promise 'real dividends in business and social advancement' which will come from ensuring that your speech and writing will be 'crisp, clear and *correct*' (their italics).

How can standard English be defined?

Linguists, unlike purveyors of English programmes, might argue with the notion of there being one 'correct' form of English grammar. Linguists recognise that there is more than one grammar of English: for example, each variety of regional English has a grammar, a set of rules understood and practised by the users of the dialect, though the rules are not written down. It is true that there is one form of English, referred to as 'standard English', which is perceived as having higher status than the others. Standard English has been defined (LINC 1992, p.355) as

> that variety of English which is usually used in print and which is normally taught in schools and to non-native speakers using the language. It is also the variety which is normally spoken by educated people and used in news broadcasts and other similar situations.[2]

It is likely that those people who feel uneasy about their own language are aware that there are some usages in their spoken, if not in their written, English which deviate from what is regarded as 'standard English'.[3]

Non-standard varieties of English, or regional dialects, are characterised by grammatical features and vocabulary which are typical of a particular geographical area. Standard English is also regarded by linguists such as David Crystal (1988) as a dialect, but not a regional one. It is associated with upper- and middle-class social groups particularly, but it affects everyone because of its official status and widespread use, especially in the written form.

Varieties of standard English

Standard English itself takes a variety of forms, with standard American English being different from standard Scottish English and standard Australian English. The variants of standard English, like all forms of language, are constantly changing and evolving. Though syntactic patterns don't change very rapidly, vocabulary is always being added or, in the case of words like 'frock' or 'wireless', is disappearing from use. There is more to linguistic change than just vocabulary however. Styles of speaking and writing, what people consider appropriate usages for any text they find themselves constructing, are to some extent like styles of dressing or home decorating. They change much more rapidly than one might think. Here, for example, is Rollo Spencer, an upper-class, successful city business man, in *The Weather in the Streets*, written in 1936 by Rosamund Lehmann. He is expressing his concern to the book's heroine, Olivia, on hearing that her father is very ill:

> I say, I'm most terribly sorry. Why didn't you tell me? How awful for you ...
> I do hope you'll find it isn't so bad ... I expect he'll be all right, honestly I do.
> Daddy was most frightfully ill last winter – heart and kidneys and God knows
> what – all the works. They said he'd never be able to shoot or fish again, and
> have to live in an arm-chair if he ever left his bed again – and now you should
> see him. He's as right as rain – practically ... Do give him my love if he remem-
> bers me ... I do wish there was something I could do ... Might I ring up?
> Would it be a bore?

I must confess that upper-class city business men are not a group of people with whom I frequently find myself engaged in creating a text of any kind, but I find it hard to imagine that the sympathy would be expressed in quite the same terms today.

As a general principle, fluidity and change in language is to be welcomed rather than feared or disapproved of, a sign of lively minds constantly seeking for new ways to express themselves. From time to time of course each of us may cringe at some aspect of language use which offends us, but this should not send us harking nostalgically back to some non-existent golden age of English.

A dialect continuum

The influence of the mass media – offering everyone the opportunity to hear and read a variety of forms of English – and increased job mobility are two of the factors which account for the fact that many people today operate on a dialect continuum, choosing and assembling their words according to whom they are speaking to, where and for what purpose. Even when speakers are at what might be thought of as 'the dialect end' of their personal speech continuum, it would be a mistake to think that in this day and age the grammar or vocabulary they use will be very different from the grammar of standard English. A few years ago, an old man who lived in Huddersfield, in West Yorkshire, told a colleague of mine:

> Well, I remember this fellow telling me that his grandfather told him that in his
> day, you could tell a Holmfirth man from a Honley man, a Honley man from,
> say, Lockwood or Berry Brow and Huddersfield – all the way down the valley

the dialect differed. You know, there was a subtle difference, and I remember George and I were producing a sort of pageant over at Slaithwaite and … they didn't know what 'laiking' was over there. The young people said, 'Well, – what's laiking?' What do you mean when you say laiking'? It's an old dialect word for 'play' isn't it?

You might find it interesting to try to collect some examples of dialect usage from your own area, though you may have to ask older members of the community, particularly for examples of vocabulary.

- In West Yorkshire, for example, it might still be possible to find someone who has just got off a crowded bus, who might say 'We were fair thrussen up' (crowded together).
- Forms of the second person singular pronouns, 'thee' and 'thou' can still be heard in Barnsley, in South Yorkshire, as in 'What does tha mean by that?'
- Non-standard uses of the verb 'to be' are fairly widespread in parts of the north: 'I were waiting two hours for a bus this morning!'
- In some parts of Lancashire, it is common for people to use a non-standard past participle for 'to sit' and 'to stand': 'I was sat [or 'were sat'] watching the film …' or 'I was stood at the window …'
- Other non-standard usages which have survived include the double negative frequently heard in south London, amongst other places: 'I don't know nothing about that.'

The examples I have given here come from my own first-hand experience, as I have moved around the British Isles because of education or jobs. You can find a more systematic account of surviving examples of regional grammars in Trudgill (1990) Again, let me stress that there is a lot of common ground as regards both grammar and vocabulary which all dialects share, though some dialects seem to have retained more distinctive features than others.

Accent

It is important to be clear that dialect, which refers to varieties of grammar and vocabulary, is not the same thing as accent. Accent refers to the ways in which speakers pronounce the sounds of English. Someone with a Lancashire accent, for example, will probably make no distinction between the /oo/ sounds in 'cook' and 'moon'. The 'a' in 'path' may sound like the 'a' in 'man'. It is perfectly possible to speak standard English with a regional accent.

Received pronunciation

Just as standard English is a high-prestige variant and usage of it tends to be associated, in many people's minds, with power and status, so there is an accent, received pronunciation (RP) which has no regional connotations, and is associated with, for example, BBC newsreaders or television commentators on grand state occasions. It's possible that some readers may associate this accent with adjectives like 'posh' or 'plummy'. Whereas it would generally be considered advisable to try to use standard English when attending a job interview, to use received pronunciation runs some risk of attracting a hostile, 'Who does she think she is?' reception. The number of people who speak RP or something close to it is much smaller than the number of speakers and writers of standard English.

Accent as an emotive issue

Reactions to accent are another fascinating area for further study, should you have the opportunity. You will be aware of how producers of television commercials are adept at choosing a suitable accent to sell their products – rural accents, such as those of Dorset or Somerset to sell wholesome products, such as brown bread; French accents for expensive perfumes; German or Japanese accents to sell cars! Attitudes and prejudices towards accents are quite illogical but often firmly entrenched, with rural accents tending to condemn their owners to being seen as slow (but trustworthy) or urban accents labelled 'ugly'. It's not unusual for those of my students who have Liverpool accents to find themselves labelled 'football hooligans', though they may never have been within half a mile of Anfield. This is one example of the responses we have learned to associate with the accents: they have nothing to do with the quality of the sounds which come out of the speakers' mouths, much less with the characteristics of those who utter them.

Substandard forms of English

You need to be aware that the term 'non-standard', which I have used to describe regional varieties of English, is sometimes applied to language which has no particular roots in history, as dialects have, but which results from carelessness, as for example when people say 'I'll have one of them books', or 'I should of done it years ago'. The term 'non-standard' is then being used as a polite variant of 'substandard'. Slang also lies outside the standard/non-standard dichotomy. Standard English speakers use slang, and regions have slang terms familiar to those who live there. The term refers to expressions which come and go very quickly, more often used in speech than in writing. They are indicative of those who use them being members of various groups, possibly age groups, social groups, or groups who spend a lot of time together in shared activities. One of the features which most obviously dates Rollo Spencer, in the book I quoted earlier, is his use of slang expressions: 'Daddy was most frightfully ill ... he's as right as rain ...' To be still using these expressions today almost certainly marks one out as being over 40.

There are suggestions for further reading on varieties of English in the chapter notes.[4] The rest of what I shall have to say in this chapter refers to the spoken and written language systems of standard English.

Section 3: The grammars of speech and of writing are not identical[5]

Some characteristics of speech

The grammar of speech and of writing are by no means identical, though obviously there are large areas of overlap. If speech is planned and rehearsed, it frequently takes on more of the characteristics of writing. Spontaneous speech on the other hand, is put together too quickly for very much consideration to be given to syntactical choices.

Ellipsis

Frequently, when speakers are talking quickly and spontaneously, some parts of the sentence are omitted.

- Want some?
- I'd like to help you but I can't.

It would be a mistake to think of these as being examples of how speech is 'sloppy' or 'more careless' than writing. In some contexts, it would make one sound very odd, even unfriendly, to say 'Would you like some tea?', though there may be formal contexts where a speaker would choose that option. It's frequently the case that speakers don't use whole sentences, when the context is an informal one. In these cases the 'units of language' which go to make up the text are known as 'utterances'. In the second example, which is a sentence, though an incomplete one, the meaning of the second half of the sentence is quite clear by referring back to the first half. This looking back to find the meaning is called 'anaphoric reference'. It would make a text sound very tedious, indeed, rather ridiculous, if everything was always stated in full: 'I'd like to help you but I can't help you.' In grammatical description, this shortening of sentences is referred to as 'ellipses'. Elided forms of words also frequently occur in speech, such as 'I'd' and 'can't' in the second example. 'Elision' is the term which refers to the omission of sounds in connected speech.

False starts

False starts are common in spontaneous speech, as the speaker realises that an utterance or a sentence is going in the wrong direction.

- We thought we might, well, would it be a good idea to …

The 'well' signals in this case that a change of direction is coming. It gives the speaker a fractional bit of thinking time.

Another way of changing direction, common in some speech contexts but not acceptable in writing, is in a sentence like the following.

• You know that girl who used to live next door, I saw her in the supermarket.

Fillers

There are other 'words' or sounds which provide speakers with a bit of time to think, like 'um' and 'er'.

I've spoken about the speed with which a spontaneous text is built up, with several people taking turns. An additional advantage of fillers is that they enable a speaker to hang on to their turn, to refuse to relinquish the conversational ball, so to speak.

Writing, as pointed out in the text chapter, can sometimes be dashed off in a way that makes it sound very like spontaneous speech. Some children tend to cling to forms of written syntax which are not very different from those of speech. If grammar is to be taught successfully in primary schools, one of the goals must be to enable children to feel confident to produce a wider range of sentence patterns, including the more literary ones that would sound most peculiar being uttered by someone standing at a bus stop. It would be unusual, for example, for a speaker, at least in ordinary conversation, to use this style of sentence construction:

> Long ago when the world was brand new, before animals or birds, the sun rose into the sky and brought the first day.   (Hughes 1963)

Section 4: Putting sentences together

What is involved in constructing a sentence? Sentences are much more difficult to define than we sometimes lead children to believe. It's easy to describe one as 'beginning with a capital letter and ending with a full stop', but this gives little or no help with the difficult question of what comes in between these two.

Sentences, whether spoken or written, fulfil four functions. They can be used

• to make statements
• to ask questions
• to utter exclamations
• to give instructions (or these might be expressed more strongly as orders or commands).

All of these can be either positive or negative.

Sentences are classified into three types:

- simple
- compound
- complex.

Experienced writers and speakers will try to match the shape of their sentences to the meanings they are trying to express.

Simple sentences

The word 'simple' is not used in grammar with a meaning akin to 'unsophisticated', nor does it imply anything about the length of the sentence. It is a technical term meaning that the sentence only contains one of each of the basic sentence requirements:

- a subject (someone or something the speaker or writer wants to focus on)
- some kind of activity associated with the subject (though the activity might be a mental activity like 'being' or 'thinking').

Speculations on the origins of sentences[6]

No one knows for sure how language began, but it is tempting to imagine some of our early ancestors using their emergent language skills to label significant aspects of their environment, such as 'Lion!' This is not of much use, however, unless you can tell people what the lion is doing: 'The lion is coming!' or 'The lion is eating Ashok!'

Types of sentence

These examples represent two very common sentence types.

- The first consists of a subject (the lion) and a part of the verb 'to come' (is coming). Though not particularly informative, the sentence is grammatically complete.
- The second sentence has another element: there is a subject ('the lion' again), an activity ('is eating') and this time, something that is being eaten (the unfortunate 'Ashok'). This last element in the sentence is called the direct object. The direct object is the person or thing on the receiving end of the activity.

Verbs are the class of words used to say what the activity in the sentence is: those followed by a direct object are called transitive verbs and the others are intransitive.

SVO (subject/verb/object) sentences

It's quite unusual to find very short sentences with only a subject (not described at all), a verb and an object (again with no information about it). Even in the speech of young children, more words are woven in, giving extra information. One place where these minimal sentences *are* frequently found is in the early levels of reading schemes, and, because it's rare to find these sentence structures in everyday life, this gives those texts their rather odd sound. Here is an example from the Ginn reading scheme, *All Aboard*, but almost all reading schemes will use the same minimalist sentence structures in the early levels. *The Parrot*, a stage one introductory text, has a series of statements with the same subject each time, 'Sam', the same verb, 'saw', and a series of direct objects.

> Sam saw a parrot.
> Sam saw a flag.
> Sam saw a sword.
> Sam saw a hat.
> Sam saw a pirate.
> Sam saw Rosie.

In *Jabeen and the New Moon* in the same scheme, Jabeen remains the subject throughout, though you will notice that she is referred to as 'she' after the first page. 'Saw' is the verb again, until we get to the last page, but as before, we have a variety of direct objects.

> Jabeen saw her new kameez.
> She saw her new shalwar.
> She saw her new sandals.
> She saw her new bangles.
> She saw the new moon.
> She put on her new clothes!

Though the text still sounds odd, judged in terms of 'real' text such as we might find in every day life, just the shift from 'Jabeen' to 'she' helps to make it sound a little bit more natural. The writer's prime purpose in writing the text in this rather monotonous way is presumably to emphasise the subject, verb, direct object sentence pattern for readers who are still at an early stage in understanding sentence structure.

SVC (subject/verb/complement) sentences

If the activity in the sentence is represented by part of the verb 'to be' the situation is rather different.

- Rosie is Sam's sister.
- Nog is our dog.
- Tomorrow might be warm and sunny.
- She was the director.

Here, 'Rosie' and 'Sam's sister' are different ways of naming the same object. 'Nog' and 'our dog' are one and the same. In the last two sentences a 'state of being' is described rather than an activity. In sentences like these four, the words that come after any part of the verb 'to be' are described not as the direct object, but the complement. This is not a complete description of the complement element in a sentence. Readers who would like to find out more will find further information in the books listed in the chapter notes.

The building blocks of sentences

Nouns

What kinds or 'classes' of words can do the job of being the subject , the object or the complement in a sentence? Very often this function is fulfilled by words behaving as nouns. Nouns are the words used by speakers and writers to name people, things, actions and ideas. Nouns can be grouped into two divisions: proper and common. Common nouns can be 'count' or 'noncount' types, and both of these types can provide concrete or abstract examples. A proper noun is the name of a specific person or a place or perhaps a special time, like 'Easter'. Proper nouns are written with a capital letter. 'Jabeen' is an example of a proper noun, and 'Sam' and 'Rosie'. Count nouns refer to individual items such as parrots, or swords, or shalwars. Noncount nouns refer to an undifferentiated mass such as sunshine. An abstract noun is something you can't see or touch, such as 'courage', 'anger' or 'loyalty'. Because I am quoting from books for beginner readers, not surprisingly these passages contain no abstract nouns.

Pronouns

We have seen how odd it sounds in *The Parrot* to mention Sam time and time again. In *Jabeen and the New Moon* 'Jabeen' was quickly replaced by 'she'. This is an example of a class of words called pronouns, which, as the name suggests, can work 'on behalf of' nouns. The pronouns are a large and quite complex class of words. Very often, the ones which stand in as the subject or object of a sentence are a subgroup called personal pronouns. They are used more frequently than any other types of pronoun.

There are pronouns 'in the first person' which allow the speaker(s) or writer(s) to include themselves in what is being said:

- I, me, myself
- we, us, ourselves.

The sentence 'We like dressing up as pirates' is written in the first person plural.

If a writer or speaker wants to address someone directly, it's possible to use a pronoun 'in the second person'. Second person pronouns include:

- you, yourselves.

An example of a sentence using a second person pronoun is: 'Do you like dressing up?' This direct address to the reader is frequently employed in books for young children.

The third person allows speakers or writers to refer to things apart from themselves or the person(s) being addressed:

- he, him, himself
- she, her, herself, it, itself
- they, them, themselves.

It must be clear to readers to whom the 'he', 'she', 'they' or 'it' refers. Usually, the noun to which the pronoun refers has been mentioned earlier in the text: 'Jabeen saw her new kameez. She saw her new shalwar. She saw her new sandals.' We know that the 'she' in the second and third sentences is the same person as 'Jabeen' in the first sentence.

Adjectives

Most listeners or readers are greedy for information, and frequently would like to know more about the subject or the object, or more about the action that is being carried out. In *Jabeen and the New Moon* 'her' and 'new' are the words which give us more information about the kameez, the shalwar, the sandals, the bangles, the moon and the clothes. They are adjectives. They can help to make the text more precise, as for example when they give

- numbers or amounts of things: three, several, many, lots
- the colour: red, vivid, rainbow-hued
- the feel: fluffy, smooth, hard-edged.

But they are dangerous things. Include too many of them, and a text can quickly sound cluttered and overwritten. I urged you in the text chapter to see reading as an interactive process, with the readers doing a lot of the work of meaning making by bringing their own ideas and associations to bear. Too many adjectives can make this difficult, constraining readers from making a personal response. Children should be advised to use this class of words sparingly and thoughtfully.

The definite and indefinite article

On the front cover of *The Parrot*, the first word, 'the', is an example of the definite article. To use it with 'parrot' indicates that the writer wants us to think of a specific parrot, a particular one. She is not going to write about parrots in general. It would be important then, with young readers, for teachers to spend time discussing the title page. Here we have *The Parrot* again, and now something which is hinted at on the front cover is more clearly discernible: the parrot is attached to a stick and is being held in someone's hand. We, the readers, are now in possession of some important information, which is reinforced by the first page of the story proper. This page is a little bit confusing because it seems to show four parrots on sticks. Most children would need help with understanding the text convention here. There are not actually four parrots but 'the' parrot being wiggled about. Sam, the main character in the story, does not have the knowledge that we the readers have. On the second page of the story, we see the parrot, but the hand and the stick are hidden by a fence. And we are told that 'Sam saw "a" parrot'. 'A' is the indefinite article and its use usually indicates that the noun has not been mentioned already. The fact that *we* know it has puts us in a very special position. It is only at the end of the story that Sam finds out what we knew from the beginning, that 'the' parrot, the one in the title, the only one the author is concerned about, belongs to Rosie, as do all the other pirate trappings that Sam has caught glimpses of.

The last sentence is 'Sam saw Rosie'. We have an example of 'zero articles' here. We would only put 'a' or 'the' with proper nouns in very special circumstances, as in:

I saw Rosie.
Do you mean the Rosie who is Sam's sister?
No, not that Rosie, the Rosie who is in our class.

Articles in generalising statements

One of the important things about certain types of non-fiction writing, such as reports, is that they frequently deal with a class of things in general, rather than named examples. It's possible then that such a piece would have zero articles in the title, which might be 'Whales', for example. The writer might then go on perhaps to use the indefinite article: 'A whale eats ...', 'A whale lives ...', though 'the whale' could alternatively be used, not in the sense of one whale, called Willy, but referring to the whole class of these creatures: 'The whale is a fascinating mammal ...'

Adverbs

I have mentioned already that not all verbs take a direct object. Those that do not are called 'intransitive' verbs. Here is an intransitive verb at work, still from the introductory level of Ginn's *All Aboard*. It's in a story called *Grandad's Balloon*.

Grandad's balloon went up.
Rosie's balloon went up.
Tilak's balloon went up.
Mo's balloon went up.
Grandad's balloon went …
POP!'

We come here to an example (although a relatively simple one) of why people find grammar irritating and difficult. At first sight it might seem as if the pattern of these sentences is very similar to what we have looked at already.

Sam	saw	a parrot.
Jabeen	saw	her new kameez.
Tilak's balloon	went	up.
Grandad's balloon	went	POP!

Figure 6.1

Word order is very important in English sentences, and children become aware of this very quickly. Even when they are only at the stage of putting two words together, English-speaking children always put them in the right order: 'Biccy gone', not 'Gone biccy'. They develop a feel for what I have listed above as 'column one' words, 'column two' words and 'column three' words. Even when putting much longer sentences together, it is seldom the word order that we find difficult. The problem is not with instinctively sorting the words out into the right order, but with having an explicit understanding of the variety of words that can occupy the third column.

If the word in the third column is a direct object, it answers the question 'what?' 'Sam saw what?' 'Jabeen saw what?' We can turn the sentence round and write it another way: 'The parrot was seen by Sam'. 'The new kameez was seen by Jabeen'. In the third sentence, 'up' doesn't answer the question 'what?', but 'where?' Actually we have a difficulty with this sentence, because the subject is a balloon. Especially in the last sentence, when grandad's balloon went 'pop' it might seem to many children that 'pop' *is* answering the question 'What?' It's actually answering the question '*How* did it go?' Another way of thinking about the difference between the third column in these last two sentences is to understand that they can't be transformed as the first two can. We can't say 'Up was gone by Tilak's balloon' or 'POP was gone by grandad's balloon'. 'To go' is an intransitive verb and it is therefore not followed by a direct object. 'Up' is an adverb of place, telling us where the balloon went, and 'pop' is an adverb of manner, telling us how the balloon met its end. Adverbs, in other words, give us more information about the activity in the sentence: the traditional way of putting this is to say that they 'modify' (rather than 'describe') the verb.

Kinds of adverb

Other types of adverb which you will meet frequently are adverbs of time, such as 'yesterday' or 'later' and adverbs of reason which, as you would expect, tell us why something happened. It usually takes more than one word to give a reason for something, as in 'because I say so ...', and so I will say more about adverbs of reason when I come to phrases and clauses.

Adverbs can move about a bit!

Though we have had examples here of adverbs in the 'column three' position, they can move about in sentences depending on the emphasis that the writer wants to give. It would have been possible to write 'Up went Tilak's balloon' or 'POP! went grandad's balloon'. Writers of the early stages of reading schemes frequently seem to make an effort to keep the syntactic shape of the sentences as close as possible to that of everyday speech. All readers are helped in their reading if they can bring some previous experience to bear when they are reading. For beginner readers, their previous language experience can only be drawn either from speech or from what they have had read to them. 'Up went Tilak's balloon' is less likely to occur in everyday speech than the form in which the sentence was actually written.

Story syntax

Whilst it is helpful to have everyday sentence shapes reinforced when children begin to read, it would be unfortunate if they did not also hear and participate in the reading of texts with more varied, more literary syntax. It is sometimes all too easy to hear the relentless rhythms of 'reading scheme syntax' in some young children's writing. These are children who may have been denied the variety of sentence shapes which can be found in texts like Ted Hughes' *How the Whale Became*, which I quoted earlier. They need to be constantly reminded of the fact that grammar is not there to constrain language users, but to be adapted to their purposes.

In the opening sentence of *The Time of the Lion* (1998) Caroline Pilcher writes: 'One day while his village slept, Joseph heard a ROAR thunderclap across the wide savannah.' 'Thunderclap' is usually used as a noun, but here the writer has decided to make it a verb, with very dramatic effect. Children should be offered a rich diet of poetry and prose from writers who are not afraid to innovate and experiment, so that they can quickly come to appreciate and try out for themselves the variety of grammatical choices which are possible in English.

Section 5: Verbs

Verbs are such a large and complex word class that I have decided to give them a section to themselves. Of all the words in a sentence, the nouns and the verbs are the most vital parts. Let us go back for a moment to Ashok and his friends in their cave, threatened by that lion. It would be helpful to know if the lion was coming quickly or slowly; it might be reassuring to know that it was an old lion or a toothless lion; it would be interesting to know if it was morning or evening when the lion came. When all is said and done, however, the two vital bits of information are a) that there was a lion and b) that it was coming towards the cave, particularly as I saw this text as a speech being addressed to Ashok himself, and not as part of a sad tale told round the camp fire to frighten the little ones for years afterwards.

The infinitive

When listing verbs, to learn them in a foreign language for example, we usually find them in their infinitive or 'base' form, the form that starts with 'to': to eat, to sleep, to walk, to climb, to run, to skip, to look and so on. The word 'infinitive' implies having no ends or boundaries. The rules of English syntax on the other hand require that all sentences must have a finite form of a verb in them. Where do the boundaries come from to make the infinitive finite? The first boundary is concerned with something you have met already: the concept of 'person'.

Person

First person
In describing pronouns, earlier in this chapter, I referred to the fact that writers and speakers can structure their texts in such a way that they are describing their own actions.

- I eat cornflakes for breakfast.
- I slept till late this morning.
- I was walking along the road when I saw my friend.

This is writing or speaking in the first person, and it gives a personal slant to the text. Of course, it may be the writer or speaker and someone else who is doing these things, in which case we would have 'we' and the verb in the first person plural. Subject and verb must agree as to person (first, second or third) and number (singular or plural) in standard English, though sentences like 'I were hoping for a new job', with a singular subject but a plural verb, are heard in some dialects.

Second person

Speakers frequently, and writers quite often, want to address their listeners or readers directly, and so they will write in the second person: 'You said that you would help me.' Standard English makes no distinction between the second person singular and the second person plural, either as regards the pronoun or the form of the verb, though again in some dialects, and in texts of a certain age, 'thou' will be found for the second person singular, and a verb ending '-est', as in 'Thou makest me glad …'.

Third person

It is frequently felt to be advisable to construct a text in a more impersonal way, mentioning neither oneself nor any particular readers. Then the third person will be used, either singular or plural. This might be a noun or a pronoun, as we have seen already.

When speakers and writers have made their decisions to structure their texts in the first, second or third person, singular or plural, the verb must follow suit. For example, let us suppose a text is being written in the present tense, and the verb 'to give' is being used. Texts in the first or second person, whether singular or plural, would have the same form of the verb:

- I give …
- we give …
- you give …

However, in the third person singular, an inflectional ending must be added:

- he gives …
- she gives …
- it gives …

Once speakers or writers have elected to compose texts in the first, second ot third person, they must put in place one of the verb 'boundaries' by choosing the appropriate inflectional endings.

Tense

The second important boundary relates to tense. A speaker or writer must decide whether the text is to be in one of the forms of the present tense, or in a past tense. English has no future tense ending, but it has several ways of expressing future time. One way is to use an adverb of time, as in the sentence 'I am going tomorrow'. (For other ways, see also comments on modal verbs below.)

It is generally expected that once chosen, the tense will be maintained throughout the text, unless there is a good reason to change it. One reason might be to include some direct speech, the actual words spoken by a character in a text. Direct speech, for example, within a narrative, might be in the present tense, though the story is being told in the past.

• Goldilocks peered in at the window. 'I wonder who lives here,' she thought.

Here we have a third person singular subject, Goldilocks, and a past tense of the verb 'to peer'. It is a regular verb, and so it forms this past tense by adding the inflection '-ed'. Many English verbs are not regular. We had the verb 'to go' earlier, in the story about the balloon; there is no past form 'goed'. When Goldilocks starts to speak, she of course refers to herself in the first person singular, and the words she speaks are in a present tense, because she is 'wondering' as she is speaking.

Modality

Writers or speakers have one other choice to make as regards which finite verb form to use: one which helps them to express a judgement about the likelihood of events. They can do this by employing one of a set of verbs called 'modals'. There is a limited number of them. Crystal (1988) includes nine verbs in this class, with four more 'marginal modals'. The 'main modals' are 'will', 'would', 'shall', 'should', 'may', 'might', 'can', 'could', 'must'. Teachers and parents often try to instil in children the distinction between 'can' and 'may':

• 'Can I leave the table please?'
  'You *can*, but you *may* not.'

However, 'may' in conversational English is beginning to sound increasingly archaic. 'Can I sit here?' is much more likely to be the modal form chosen by a young person than 'May I?', and so the teacher's comment may not be understood or may at best seem rather carping.

Auxiliaries

It's frequently the case that to complete the tense of the verb they have chosen, speakers or writers must use more than one word:

			stay
		has	stayed
	had	been	staying
must	have	been	staying

A verb, even when it consists of only one word, 'stay' or 'eats' or 'reads' or 'hoped', is described as a verb phrase. This is another of those irritating aspects of grammar, because generally it helps to be able to define a phrase to children as 'a group of words acting together'. (There is more discussion of phrases in the next chapter.)

The verbs which sometimes help to make up tenses are known as auxiliary verbs. Parts of the verbs 'to be', 'to have' and 'to do' frequently function as auxiliary verbs. As you can see above, more than one auxiliary can be used at a time.

There are a number of forms of the past and present. Some grammarians call each of these 'tenses': for example, the 'perfect tense' and the 'pluperfect tense'. Crystal (1988) calls them 'aspects'. Labelling them all is not something that native speakers are usually taught to do, though you may have met these labels if you have learned another language. I don't think it would be appropriate for children at Key Stage 2 to struggle with this labelling but sometimes children may need help if they are constructing a text in the past tense but where something is further back in the text than the rest. 'Cinderella lived with her father and her ugly sisters. She had been a happy child until her mother died when she was three.' Here, the second sentence, using the auxiliary 'had', describes events which are no longer ongoing when the story starts, but are further back in time. To have written 'has been' instead would have implied that the situation was continuing into the time the story is dealing with, whereas, in fact, this situation is over before the story begins.

'-ed' and '-ing' participles

In some tenses, or 'aspects,' alongside the auxiliaries are forms of the verb which, in the case of regular verbs, carry the inflectional endings '-ed' and '-ing'. Examples are:

- has stayed
- has been staying.

The -ed participle acting as part of a verb phrase

'-ed' is an inflectional ending we have met already, forming a past tense of regular verbs: 'wanted', 'helped', 'climbed' and so on. (It's worth pointing out to children that although all these are regular past tenses, formed by adding 'ed' to the infinitive form of the verb, they don't all sound the same. We can hear /t/ in 'helped', /d/ in 'climbed' and /ed/ in 'wanted'.)

We are now meeting '-ed' forms in another guise however, working alongside an auxiliary. If we write 'He has stayed …'. the form of the verb 'stayed', which is being used with an auxiliary, 'has' to form a past tense, used to be known as the past participle. However, this terminology is confusing as this participle can be used to refer to future time also, as in: 'After tomorrow, I will have stayed at this hotel five times.'

The '-ed' participle as an adjective

The '-ed' participle can also be used as an adjective: 'the chopped tomatoes', 'the used tickets'.

These '-ed' adjectives act as a complement after any form of the verb 'to be':

- The athlete was exhausted.
- The glass was broken [not 'broked', because 'to break' is an irregular verb].

The '-ing' participle acting as part of a verb phrase

If we refer back to the list of auxiliaries above, we find another inflectional ending '-ing'. Forms of the verb which end in '-ing' have traditionally been known as present participles: 'walking', 'sleeping', 'thinking' and so on. However, they function in similar ways to '-ed' participles. They can form a part of a finite form of a verb, so long as they have auxiliaries alongside, to complete a range of tenses: 'I am walking' (present) or 'They were sleeping' (past) or 'We will be thinking' (future).

The '-ing' participle acting as an adjective

'-ing' participles , like '-ed' participles, can also act as adjectives:

- the slithering snake
- the growling dog
- the boiling kettle.

The '-ing' participle as a noun

Examples of this usage are:

- Fishing is not allowed in this river
- My favourite sport is swimming.

It is important to make it clear to children that neither '-ing' participles by themselves nor infinitives (sometimes known as 'base forms') can provide that finite verb form which every sentence must usually have. They can only fulfil this role if they have an auxiliary to help them. In the text 'Class Five were having an outing. Walking along the beach and swimming in the sea', the first sentence is grammatical, because 'having' has an auxiliary with it, to help form a past tense. The second sentence is not grammatical because the only forms of verbs which appear in it are '-ing' participles without auxiliaries, 'walking' and 'swimming'. There should be a comma after 'outing' and then 'walking' and 'swimming' can fulfil their roles as adjectives, describing 'Class Five'.

Mood

The indicative mood

So far, nearly all the examples I have given in this section on verbs have been contained in sentences which were making statements.

- The lion is coming.
- I am going tomorrow.

Most verb phrases are in the indicative mood, which is used for making statements. It can also be used for asking questions: 'The lion is coming?' The addition of a question mark tells the reader that the voice rises after coming, and the tone is questioning.

The interrogative mood

The questions 'Is the lion coming?' and 'When shall I go?' are different, because they have clear question markers inside them. In the first case, the word order reveals that a question has been asked: 'Is ... coming'. In the second, as well as the word order indication, there is also a question word 'when'. These sentences are in the interrogative mood.

The imperative mood

The imperative mood is used when a writer or speaker wants to give suggestions, or orders or instructions (the force behind the imperative will depend very much on the context). If you are doing work on lists with children, or helping them to write recipes or any kind of procedural writing, you will need to draw their attention to the ways in which sentences can be expressed, with varying degrees of force, in the imperative mood. Frequently the verb comes first, and no subject is expressed.

- Break the eggs into the bowl.
- Take a piece of string.
- Go now!

Sometimes teachers try to avoid what might seem like the harshness of the imperative mood by casting their commands or requests in the form of a question instead. 'Shall we put the books away, Robert?' is therefore possibly another way of saying 'Put the books away, Robert, please'. Robert may come unstuck at this point because he has no previous experience of requests being structured in this way. To answer 'No', or even 'No thank you', would not be appropriate.

There is another mood, the subjunctive, which enables the construction of sentences like 'If I were you, I would not waste time'. It is used very little in modern English.

Active and passive voice

As we have already seen above, writers or speakers frequently choose to empha-sise themselves or their addressee in the way they structure their sentences. They do this by making 'I/we' or 'you' the subject of their sentences. Otherwise, if a more impersonal style of writing is desired, a noun or pronoun in the third person is chosen. In each case we have noticed the pattern of a subject, followed by an activity carried out by that subject. Here is an example of a sentence with a third person singular subject, 'birds', a verb in a present tense, 'make', and a noun, 'nests', that is serving as the object of the sentence:

• Birds make nests.

The sentence is written in such a way that readers understand that the subject, the birds, are actively involved in the making. We say that this sentence is in the active voice. One of the features of subject/verb/object sentences, as we have seen already, is that the same meaning can be expressed in another way.

• Nests are made by the birds.

In this version, the 'nests' are now the subject of the sentence, but they do not actually *do* anything. They have something done to them. This sentence is in the passive voice. The birds are the 'agents'. The events are the same, but they are being described in a different way.

It is possible to have sentences in the passive voice in which the agent is not expressed.

• In spring, nests are made.

Though not particularly significant in this instance, on some occasions it can be very useful to be able to draw a veil over who or what is responsible for some-thing by omitting to mention the agent. Recently, for example, I filled in an important form for my course leader and returned it to her. Some days later, she asked me for the form again. A number of language choices were open to me. I could have said 'Have you lost the form?', but this would have been unwise. More tactful is 'Has the form been lost?' omitting any mention of an agent. Even this hints at carelessness, and so in the end I opted for 'Has the form disappeared?' As 'to disappear' is an intransitive verb, it manages to convey the idea that somehow the form lost itself (at least, I hope so).

It is time now to leave the safe shores of the simple sentence for the more difficult terrain of compound and complex sentences, where boundaries are hazy and where thickets of syntax can trap the unwary.

Pause for thought

No, I haven't gone completely mad, nor have I been drinking (it's only 11.30 in the morning). Before starting on the next chapter I am inviting you to have another pause for thought. I would like you to think about your reaction to my change of style in the sentence above. It would be useful if you have read Chapter 4, because in that chapter I raised some issues about structuring different types of text. If you are willing to pause, I would like you to ask yourselves whether you felt irritated by a piece of purple prose in the middle of a section of exploratory text. This might support the theory that genre choices are as much about meeting readers' expectations as they are about exploring writers' meanings. You were going along quite nicely following some explanations of points of grammar and syntax, when suddenly you were jolted into something you were not prepared for and which seemed as inappropriate as wearing a dinner jacket on the beach. (It is possible of course that you welcomed this break into something more colourful as a pleasing change from what had gone before.)

On the other hand, it may not be the inappropriateness of the style that you object to. It may be that you can't understand a word of what I'm talking about. What on earth do I mean by 'thickets of syntax?' You may have no mental image of a thicket, or, if you have, may not see what thickets have to do with syntax. If the chapter is to go on in this vague and imprecise way, you may feel you want none of it. In writing 'thickets of syntax' I am employing a metaphor, and I shall have more to say about their use (and abuse) in a later chapter.

One final point for you to consider before I try to resume my original explanatory style. One of the syntactic issues I have raised in this chapter is the question of writing in the first, second or third person. I have used first and second person pronouns throughout this book, and I await with interest my publisher's reactions to this. He may decide to chop them all out. Just now, I raised the interpersonal level of the writing quite a bit by telling you that I am writing this at 11.30 in the morning. I tried to force you in other words, to visualise me for a moment, instead of verbs, nouns or whatever. I would like you to consider the effect of this much more intrusive 'I' at this point in the text. On the whole, adults are meant to know enough about syntactic choices to control the level of 'I' and 'you' interference in accordance with the kind of text they are writing. Children take some considerable time to learn this.

Chapter 7

Sentence structure: phrases and clauses

In order to qualify as a sentence at all, a group of words must contain within it at least one example of a verb in a finite form. We have established in the last chapter that this means one of the forms of a verb which is bounded by tense and person. A sentence with only one finite verb in it is technically known as a simple sentence, or a one clause sentence. The fact that it is labelled 'simple' does not have anything to do with its length: not all simple sentences are like the sentences we read from the reading scheme. In *Prowlpuss*, by Gina Wilson (1994), we are introduced to the eponymous hero with a terrifying picture of a huge moggy on the first double page spread. Here is no simple opening sentence to get us off to a gentle start. Gentleness is not what this book is about. We plunge straight in with:

> Prowlpuss is cunning and wily and sly,
> A kingsize cat with one ear and one eye.
> He's not a sit-by-the-fire-and-purr cat,
> A look-at-my-exquisite-fur cat,
> No, he's not!
>
> He's rough and gruff and very very tough.
>
> Where ya goin', Prowlpuss?
>
> AHA

Adjectival phrases

English syntax has been taken by the scruff of the neck in this rhyming story and made to support the author's vivid word picture. The work of describing a noun can be done by a single adjective standing alone:

• Prowlpuss is cunning.

but by using a word class that we have not talked about yet, a writer can create a more complex picture by joining several adjectives together into adjectival phrases:

- Prowlpuss is cunning *and* wily *and* sly.

A phrase is a group of words working together as a single element in a sentence, in this case to do the work of describing a noun. So we have an adjectival phrase. There is another adjectival phrase in the same sentence, this time describing 'cat':

- with one ear and one eye.

Conjunctions

The 'ands' in that adjectival phrase belong to a class of word called conjunctions. The job of all conjunctions is to join sentences or parts of sentences together. 'And' is probably the commonest conjunction of all, though 'or' and 'but' are also frequently used.

These conjunctions are called coordinating conjunctions, because all the parts they link together have the same status in the sentence. In my example, 'cunning', 'wily' and 'sly' are all adjectives. It would be possible of course to miss out one or even both of the 'ands':

- Prowlpuss is cunning, wily and sly.

The two 'ands' are another example of an author making syntax serve her meaning: it seems to me that she is piling up the cat's character traits in a very deliberate and emphatic way.

In a spirited approach to conventional grammar which I thoroughly recommend to you, the author has invented her most effective adjectives of all by yoking words together with hyphens to make unique structures, totally unconventional grammatically, but great fun to read:

- a sit-by-the-fire-and-purr cat
- a look-at-my-exqusite-fur cat.

Later on in the text, we are told that Prowlpuss is not a

- cuddle-up-for-a-chat cat
- or a sit-in-the-window-and-stare cat
  He's an I WAS THERE! cat.

Adverb phrases

Adverb phrases work on the same principle as adjectival ones. Words are combined to do the same work as a single adverb would do. I have mentioned already that adverbs are a word class which can be moved about in a sentence to place the emphasis where the author wants it. Look at this example from later on in Prowlpuss's story:

* Back through the alley slinks Prowlpuss at dawn.

The subject of the sentence is Prowlpuss, but on this occasion, the adverb phrase, 'back through the alley' is placed first. It's an adverb phrase of place, because it tells us more about (or modifies) the verb, 'slinks'. It tells us *where the slinking was done*. Putting it first throws quite a lot of emphasis on the phrase and on the word 'slinks'. There is good reason why Prowlpuss is slinking at this point, but I don't want to give too much away.

Noun phrases

Another type of phrase which you will frequently encounter is the noun phrase. Noun phrases are groups of words, acting as a unit, which do the same work as single nouns. We have noticed already that the work nouns do is, frequently, to be the subject or the object of a sentence. Prowlpuss's owner is called Nellie Smith. Look at the sentence

* And old Nellie Smith in her deep feather bed
  Lifts her head.

The verb in the sentence is 'lifts'. It's interesting that the story is told in the present tense. The past is more usual in a narrative. You might like to speculate on the effect of using a present tense instead. Who does the lifting? Or in other words, who is the subject of the sentence? The group of words 'old Nellie Smith' is filling this slot: a group of words forming a noun phrase. (Are you able to describe what work is being done by the group of words 'in her deep feather bed'?)

Grammar supports meaning making!

I would like to think that children who are offered the kind of spirited reading material they will find in this text (and I have only talked about the grammar: there's much more to enjoy than that) will not grow up afraid of grammar's terrible teeth, but will see it as there to serve speakers and writers in their struggles to express themselves and to have fun with meaning. I cannot emphasise too strongly the importance of approaching grammar through exploring meaning. I can see little point in asking children to 'spot the phrase in line 10' or to even to 'make a list of all the adjectival phrases in the story' unless the children can see a reason for doing so. Phrase and clause boundaries are notoriously difficult to define, and I think this is too complex an activity for children in Key Stage 2. But as an adult shares the text with the class, and they enjoy together the vivid picture that is being built up, it would be possible for the adult to pick out some of the phrases, bring them to the children's attention, (explaining why they are called phrases) and then to discuss with the children how effective they are.

Compound sentences

In all the sentences I have discussed so far, there has only been one finite verb. This is why they are all defined as simple sentences. Two simple sentences or one-clause sentences can be joined together, using a conjunction. This will form a compound sentence. Each part of a compound sentence could stand alone grammatically. There are various reasons why writers or speakers may want to join them. Speakers, if they are 'in full flow', may not even be conscious that they are doing this. Loosely strung sentences, joined with 'and' or 'but' or 'or' may just pour from them. Writers have more time to think and to revise their sentence shapes. Forming compound sentences may be part of a plan to give a sentence a feeling of balance or to put two sides of a case.

Imagine that the following is the opening sentence of a story:

Little Red Riding Hood was a good girl but she really should have paid more attention to her mother's advice.

In the first part of this compound sentence, we have a subject:

• Little Red Riding Hood

and a finite verb:

• was.

In the second part, which is co-equal with the first, we have a subject:

• she (referring back to the previously mentioned 'Little Red Riding Hood')

and a finite verb:

• should have paid.

Linking the two parts together enables us to consider two facets of her character. Little Red Riding Hood is to be the heroine of the story, so we want to engage the readers' sympathies for her: on the other hand, she did have a weakness, and this is what will lead to the complication in her story.

From a non-fiction text, *Time and Space*, by Mary and John Gribbin (1994), we have another example of the way a compound sentence allows writers to hold two ideas in relation to each other. The writers have been making the point that we seem to move through – or with – time, *but* always in the same direction:

• We cannot go back for a second to look at the past, nor can we jump forward for a preview of the future.

'Nor' is the conjunction here. It is a rather literary conjunction, very seldom used in spoken English. Notice how it requires an inversion of the finite verb after it.

Children tend to use the conjunction 'and' very indiscriminately in their writing, and sometimes it's difficult to explain to them how to edit some of them out. Children in Key Stage 2 should be encouraged to justify the use of the word in their texts. If they can't find a reason for a particular 'and', it would be worth seeing whether the text sounded better without it.

Complex sentences

In order to begin to understand complex sentences, we need to return to the three word classes we have met twice before already:

• adjectives
• adverbs
• nouns.

You should by now be fairly clear about the work each of these word classes does in sentences. You will also remember that this work can be done

• by single adjectives, adverbs or nouns:
  'She has written a *simple* story.' (adjective)
  'They crept *slowly*, towards the hut.' (adverb)
  '*Jack* fell down.' (noun)
• by groups of words acting together to form a phrase:
  'She has written a simple story *with a brilliant ending*.' (adjectival phrase)
  'They crept towards the hut *on their hands and knees*.' (adverbial phrase)
  '*That good-for-nothing Jack* fell down.' (noun phrase)

Subordinate clauses

It is also possible to insert groups of words into sentences, which do the work of adverbs, adjectives and nouns, and which have their own subject and their own finite verb. Because they have a finite verb, they are not phrases, but clauses.

In complex sentences, there is only one clause which could, in theory, make sense by itself. It is known as the main clause. The other clauses are dependent upon, or relate to the main clause in some way or other. They are known as subordinate clauses.

- A complex sentence is technically a sentence with a main clause and at least one subordinate clause.

It need not be very long or 'complex' in the non-technical sense, just as a so-called 'simple' sentence can actually be quite long and involved. However, some writers are masters (or mistresses) of the complex sentence, and can weave clauses together so beautifully that half the pleasure of reading their work is in appreciating their beautiful cadences. Jane Austen is an obvious example. Here is the opening sentence from *Persuasion*:

Sir Walter Elliot, of Kellynch-hall in Somersetshire, was a man who, for his own amusement, never took up any book but the Baronetage; there he found occupation for an idle hour, and consolation in a distressed one; there his faculties were roused into admiration and respect, by contemplating the limited remnant of the earliest patents; there any unwelcome sensations, arising from domestic affairs, changed naturally into pity and contempt, as he turned over the almost endless creations of the last century – and there, if every other leaf were powerless, he could read his own history with an interest which never failed.

This kind of complex sentence would sound very odd in a spoken text, and yet it is what gives the writing its unique flavour.

Types of subordinate clause

Relative clauses

- She has written a simple story *which will delight all young readers*.

In this expanded version of what started off as a simple sentence, we now have two pieces of information about the story:

- it is simple
- it will delight all young readers.

There are two clauses because there are two finite verbs, 'has written' and 'will delight'. In this example, 'which' relates all the words which come after it to the one word 'story'. In old-fashioned clause analysis, this group of words would have been described as an adjectival phrase. Nowadays, it would be labelled a 'relative clause'. This label is more appropriate because, introduced as they are by relative pronouns, it is possible for relative clauses to do other work than describing nouns. For example, in the sentence

• He is working hard, which is a miracle

'which' relates *everything* which comes after it, to *everything* which has gone before.

Relative clauses can also be introduced by the relative pronouns 'who' and 'that'.

• Susan, who is my mother's cousin, has gone to live in Australia.
• This is the book that I told you about.

In both of these examples, the relative clauses are giving more information about nouns, 'Susan' and 'book'. In these particular cases they are therefore acting adjectivally.

Adverbial clauses

Subordinate adverbial clauses do similar work to adverbs and adverbial phrases. The sentence 'They crept towards the hut' makes perfect sense as it stands. It could be a one clause sentence. However, the person writing this text would probably feel under pressure to explain why this unusual activity was taking place: 'They crept towards the hut because they were afraid of being seen'. The one clause sentence has now become the main clause of a complex sentence, and a subordinate clause has been added.

This second clause, because it does the work of explaining why the 'creeping' was going on, is an adverbial clause of reason. Like its cousin, the single adverb, it can move about in the sentence, depending on where the writer wants to put the emphasis: 'Because they were afraid of being seen, they crept towards the hut' is just as acceptable grammatically, though many inexperienced readers find it difficult to cope with sentences where too many words come before the main subject. To be able to cope with and enjoy the effect of sentences like the latter version, is another test of a child's developing literary prowess.

Noun clauses

There is one other form of subordination that you need to be aware of, where the subordinate clause fulfils a role similar to that done by nouns or pronouns.

• I said those words.
• I said *that you may go to the party.* (object)

• It is not important.
• *What you did* is not important. (subject)

- Take it to her.
- Take it to *whoever is waiting for it.*

Clauses in context

I would advocate the same approach to work on clauses as I have suggested for phrases. 'Spotting the clauses' is meaningless, unless there is some discussion linked to their use. In the following extract from *The Lion, the Witch and the Wardrobe* (1950) C.S. Lewis is establishing the first setting for his fantasy story, the house from which the children will pass through into Narnia.

> It was the sort of house that you never seem to come to the end of, and it was full of unexpected places. The first few doors they tried led only into spare bedrooms, as everyone had expected that they would; but soon they came to a very long room full of pictures and there they found a suit of armour; and after that was a room all hung with green, with a harp in one corner; and then came three steps down and five steps up, and then a kind of little upstairs hall and a door that led out on to a balcony, and then a whole series of rooms that led into each other and were lined with books – most of them very old books and some bigger than a Bible in a church. And shortly after that they looked into a room that was quite empty except for one big wardrobe; the sort that has a looking-glass in the door. There was nothing else in the room at all except a dead blue-bottle on the window sill.
>
> 'Nothing there!' said Peter, and they all trooped out again – all except Lucy.

There's quite an array of 'ands' here, but all thoroughly justified. No one would want to list all the phrases and clauses, but what we can do is to draw the passage to children's attention, and show them how well the sentence structure matches the house the writer is describing. For example, the second sentence, which is very long indeed, matches with its twists and turns the twisting passages and the rooms leading off one another which characterise the building. Punctuation is vital to prevent the reader from getting lost in the sentence: it contains three semi-colons, four commas and a hyphen!

When we come to the next sentence, (the one beginning with 'and'!) we have quite a different structure, where a few phrases are allowed to stand out sharply:

- quite empty
- one big wardrobe.

The next sentence is even more stark in its simplicity:

- There was nothing else in the room at all. [Except for the dead blue-bottle which is a touch of genius, I think. It doesn't detract from the stark simplicity, but adds to it.]

The word 'nothing' in that sentence is picked up again, and reinforced, when it is put into the mouth of Peter – and so we as readers are on a knife edge: will the magic be discovered or not?

To talk about the writer's skill in weaving different sentence structures together is very different from picking out the clauses with highlighter pen, a difficult and soul-destroying task. The children can be introduced to the jargon:

* phrase
* clause
* simple sentence
* compound sentence
* complex sentence.

But the most important aspect of the discussion is to appreciate what a skilful writer can do with these structures. It may also be that some children will be encouraged to have a go at a more deliberate use of subordinate clauses themselves as a result of such explicit discussion, or may be helped to see how they can increase the flow of their sentences by incorporating some of the information they want to convey in subordinate clauses.

Cohesion and connection

Grammar, as I have been at pains to explain in this chapter and the last, is the speaker's or writers' tool, enabling meaning to be structured and expressed in a variety of subtle ways. Though some indulgence is shown to speakers if speed and spontaneity render them a little bit incoherent, writers and indeed speakers who have time to rehearse will go to some trouble to make their texts 'cohesive' or, in other words, to ensure that each bit of their meaning is somehow bound into the whole so that readers or listeners can follow their drift, and can see the connections between one sentence or one part of the text and another. I can illustrate this by asking you to look back at the extract from *The Lion, the Witch and the Wardrobe*.

Conjunctions

Conjunctions come immediately to mind when we think of joining parts of a text together, and indeed they are important, though they are by no means the only way of forming cohesive links. In the first sentence of the extract for example, C.S. Lewis provides two pieces of information about the house, both of equal importance, so he links them together with 'and'.

* It was the sort of house that you never seem to come to the end of, and it was full of unexpected places.

Sometimes, the writer wants to provide contrastive information, and so 'but' is a more useful conjunction.

• The first few doors they tried led only into spare bedrooms, as everyone had expected that they would; but soon they came to a very long room full of pictures ...

Adverbs as cohesive ties

Adverbs provide strong links in a text, allowing a variety of connections between items. Here they are largely temporal, though there is one spatial connection:

• soon they came to a very long room ... (temporal link)
• after that there was a room ... (ditto)
• and then came ... (ditto)
• and then a kind of ... (ditto)
• and then a whole series ... (ditto)
• shortly after that ... (ditto)
• there they found a suit of armour ... (spatial link)

Pronouns

Pronouns allow writers to make referential connections back to people or things mentioned already earlier in the text:

• it [the house] was full of unexpected places. The first few doors they [the children] tried led only into spare bedrooms.

Ellipsis

Sometimes words, or even longer parts of sentences, can be omitted, because the writer assumes that his readers will carry some meaning forward:

• one big wardrobe; the sort ['of wardrobe' omitted] that has a looking glass in the door.
• The first few doors ... led only into spare bedrooms, as everyone had expected that they would ['lead' omitted].

Lexical cohesion

Words can be repeated, exemplifying one type of what is known as lexical cohesion:

• rooms that led into each other and were lined with books – most of them very old books and some ['books' omitted] bigger than a Bible in a church.

Another type of lexical cohesion is represented by the 'books ... Bible' link. Writers can achieve cohesiveness in their texts by using words which collocate, or 'keep company with each other' (for more on collocation, see p.91).

Readers must work hard to make cohesive links

Writers come to expect a fair amount of skill and expertise from readers, with regard to such things as filling the gaps left by elided meanings, looking back to find a referent previously mentioned, or carrying a word or phrase forward in the mind until it is referred to a little while later in the text. The nature of the cohesive ties will very much depend on the type of text. In a recipe, for example, some of the cohesion might be provided by numbering each stage in the process. Sometimes, writers delight in omitting cohesive ties, leaving the reader with a lot of detective work to do. This wealth of connectives and cohesive ties can take some time for children to become familiar with in reading, let alone to make use of in their own texts. (For suggestions of further reading on connectives and cohesion, please see the books suggested in the notes for Chapters 6 and 7.)

It would be impossible in two chapters to explore all the highways and byways of English grammar. There are those who delight in arguing over a particular usage or analysing an obscure example. This is to make grammar an end in itself and for some it is a life's work. In primary schools, I think the task is not to seek out the difficult or the obscure example, but to make clear the basic principles on which text is constructed, in the hope that this will serve the more important ends of meaning making and sharing.

Chapter 8

Words, words, words

Ask someone what they think of as 'language development' and vocabulary is likely to be one of the first things they mention. When I ask new students – or children – why we learn to read, frequently the first reason either group give is 'to learn new words' (from the children) or 'to increase our vocabulary' (might be the way the students put it). When I look at the aims listed in the language policies of some schools, I often see the same priority. Here is a typical policy:

> As language is so important when working with young children our aims are to:
>
> - develop a good vocabulary
> - encourage them to articulate and speak clearly
> - help them to acquire the ability to retell and explain what they are doing
> - be able to repeat rhymes and stories
> - use their imaginations to tell their own stories
> - learn how to hold a conversation with friends and adults – listen as well as talk
> - explain how they feel
> - express their own opinions.

These are all worthwhile language aims, but I would like to turn them round a bit and to combine the elements in different ways.[1] The sixth point holds the key to it all.

Starting from an interesting context

As young children build up confidence in conversing, first with family and friends and then with a wider circle of adults, explaining how they feel, expressing their own opinions, listening to others as well as talking, they will find more and more things to talk about. They may talk about where they have been, about something they have been told, or about what they have seen on television. They may try out some of the words they have heard others use, they will receive feedback and extension of their ideas from supportive adults and hence, gradually, they will develop a wider vocabulary – words that they can use again and again. This vocabulary will largely be of the 'everyday' sort: the nouns, verbs, adjectives and so on that we use to gossip, to mull over events, to describe our plans, to make requests and so on.

Finding the 'right' words[2]

Building up their everyday vocabulary is not without its difficulties and dangers for some children. Precisely because a word seems so ordinary, so rooted in everyday experience for an adult, he or she may be proportionately more outraged by a child who uses a different word. I have never forgotten a discussion I had with a teacher from a South Yorkshire school who was adamant that no child in her class was going to write under her picture 'This is me playing with my mates', though this is an everyday word for 'friends' in that area. Children are often criticised for using vocabulary that seems to a teacher limited or regional or impolite – as in the requests for going to the toilet mentioned on p.32. I remember another angry teacher declaring 'I will not have them coming in in the morning and saying "Wotcher, miss!"'

This is not to deny a teacher the right to negotiate in his or her classroom how greetings, requests for the toilet, etc. will be expressed. But it is a plea for careful and sympathetic handling of these issues. The vocabulary of school can require some getting used to, as can the need to be more explicit and to speak more clearly and distinctly than is often necessary at home. However, the urge to join in these everyday classroom conversations will be a powerful incentive to get the pitch and volume to the acceptable standard, to remember to look someone in the eye, and to smile at the right moment. All these add up to a complex set of expectations and take some time to get right. Many an adult has never done so.

Shared worlds, shared words

The words we use to talk or write to people we know well are deeply rooted in shared experience. One word in such a context can carry as much meaning as a dozen words to someone we scarcely know. Children have been part of these shared implicit meanings since they were born, but it will take some time before they are conscious of how the degree of explicitness when dealing with a topic must be adjusted depending on the context and the audience.

The words of songs and rhymes

So far, I have been talking about spoken vocabulary of an unrehearsed kind – used in those contexts where speech is very different from writing. In addition to these words, some children will come to school knowing words they have learned in rhymes and counting games. Some will already have a repertoire of favourite songs and stories. Teachers need to build on these experiences so that all the children meet words of another sort from the everyday ones:

- Ring a ring o' roses, a pocket full of posies
- Hickory, dickory, dock
- Little Miss Muffett sat on her tuffett.

They may not be sure what some of these words mean. What exactly happened to Jack when he fell down and 'broke his crown?' What, for that matter, was the 'pail' of water he went up the hill to fetch? But in these cases, not knowing the exact meaning of the words does not spoil the pleasure of joining in the songs and rhymes: the words will largely be used in the specific context of singing or reciting. It may never come to light that the meanings are a bit of a mystery.

Words encountered in stories

Favourite stories are a different case again. Here, we do all want to share in the meanings that are being explored, but the words that are used are often not the same as the ones for everyday use, or if they are, they are combined in ways different from those heard at the breakfast table or the bus stop:

> Once upon a time, there was a dark, dark moor. On the moor was a dark, dark wood. In the wood, there was a dark, dark house. At the front of the house, there was a dark, dark door …   (Brown 1981)

A tired parent, wanting to get out of reading a bed time story, might try to get away with a retelling: 'We've had this one before: you remember there was a box, in a corner of a cupboard, behind a curtain, along a passage …' It just won't do. What we have here is not a boring repetitious use of the word 'dark'; here we have the opportunity to scare ourselves witless, even though we've heard the story many times before and we know there's only a mouse at the end. The repetition of the word, together with the wonderful illustrations, works on us like a spell.[3]

Words can't come out of nothing

To return to the views with which I opened this chapter: it is unwise to see the growth of vocabulary as a first priority in language development. What we are dealing with here is another example of the necessity for a 'top-down' perspective on the growth of language knowledge. Vocabulary – whether of the everyday, bread and butter variety, or of the more literary kinds – grows slowly out of experience – experience of talking and listening and reading, and then experimenting with writing. If the experience has been a good one, or a challenging one, making new demands on us, we are more likely to remember some of the new words which helped us to come to terms with it. But there is little or no chance of remembering any words if the experience was contrived. There is even less likelihood if no experience at all was provided, and the word work was merely part of a set of decontextualised language exercises. What do I mean by a contrived experience? The teacher who responds to a spring morning by asking the children for all the words they can think of to describe it, writes the words on the board, and then encourages the class to incorporate as many of these words as possible into a poem, is unlikely to add very much to any pupil's permanent vocabulary.

Drama and role play

To emphasise the quality of experience does not necessarily mean that all the experience must be first hand. It is very difficult, for example, to give children first-hand experience of finding the appropriate vocabulary to negotiate with powerful adults. Role play is one way of doing it.[4] Through improvised drama after a shared story, children can be required, for example, to conjure up the words to persuade the cowardly king to lead his army into battle. Film and television are likely to offer today's children some of their most powerful experiences – and of course, reading and being read to. In choosing to share any of these with children, the criterion uppermost in our minds should not be the growth in vocabulary that may result, but the quality of the experience that the text, whether media text or written, provides. We want to know more about space, or dinosaurs, or King Henry VIII. We want to know how to look after guinea pigs. We want to give ourselves a thrill or a fright or a good laugh. Quality texts can offer all of these and will at the same time provide new words for our consideration.

The danger of working from extracts

There is some danger, in the approach advocated by the National Literacy Strategy, of plundering a text for suitable extracts in order to explore aspects of grammar or vocabulary, perhaps in order to discuss how a character has been delineated or a setting described. This is not the intention, but it may nevertheless be an unfortunate outcome, and we would then be back to something akin to the decontextualised exercise. In the training materials for Module 5, *Shared and Guided Reading and Writing at Key Stage 2 (Fiction and Poetry)*, teachers are advised that 'In planning for fiction within the Literacy Hour you should aim to use extracts from longer, high-quality children's novels for Shared Reading wherever possible. *You will probably be reading these as class novels outside the Literacy Hour*' (p.5, my italics). Though it's not part of my brief to discuss classroom approaches in this book, I would like to make it clear how important I think this last sentence is. I can see little merit in offering children isolated extracts from a text. The child needs to start from the experience of the film or the book as a whole. If a book is to be the basis of the shared work, it may be read aloud by the teacher and may be edited to fit into a certain number of shared reading sessions. Some children may be encouraged to read it independently and to read other texts for comparison and contrast. We can help children to become more explicitly aware of how writers achieve their effects through skilful use of text structure, sentence shapes and choice of words. But in 'numbering the streaks on the tulip' we must be very careful indeed that we don't lose sight of the whole flower. Having made my position clear, I hope, I can now go on to show how an interest in words and an enthusiasm for trying them out in one's own work, might grow from shared reading of quality texts.

Word level work based on *The Wind in the Willows*

I mentioned the possibility of writing about spring earlier in this chapter. There is an opportunity to look closely at how an established children's author, Kenneth Grahame, has tackled this in *The Wind in the Willows* (1908). In Chapter 1, Mole has emerged from a heavy bout of spring cleaning and is going for a walk.

> It all seemed too good to be true. Hither and thither through the meadows he rambled busily, along the hedgerows, across the copses, finding everywhere birds building, flowers budding, leaves thrusting – everything happy and progressive and occupied … He thought his happiness was complete when, as he meandered aimlessly along, suddenly he stood by the edge of a full-fed river. Never in his life had he seen a river before – this sleek, sinuous, full-bodied animal, chasing and chuckling, gripping things with a gurgle and leaving them with a laugh, to fling itself on fresh playmates that shook themselves free and were caught and held again. All was a-shake and a-shiver – glints and gleams and sparkles, rustle and swirl, chatter and bubble.

Synonyms, connotation and denotation[5]

One place to start thinking about this text at the word level might be with the words Kenneth Grahame has used instead of 'going for walk.' We are first of all told that Mole

• rambled busily.

Later on he

• meandered aimlessly.

'Ramble' and 'meander' are synonyms of 'walk.' A synonym is defined as a word that means the same as another. In fact, no two words ever do mean exactly the same thing to a native speaker. Their dictionary or 'lexical' meaning may be the same. That is, they may label or 'denote' the same activity, quality or object. In this case, the words denote putting one foot in front of another and moving along. The denotation of words is probably their least interesting aspect, however. As we read this passage, Mole first rambling and then meandering will conjure up for each reader different ways of 'putting one foot in front of another and moving along'. That is to say, the words will have a variety of connotations, or personal associations for each of us. This will depend to some extent on our age, interests, attitudes to walking and so on. Of course, among readers who share a social and cultural background, there are likely to be a lot of shared connotations.

Kenneth Grahame has elaborated on the two synonyms, 'rambled' and 'meandered', by adding adverbs after them. Mole 'rambled busily' and he 'meandered aimlessly'. This to some extent controls the readers' reactions more tightly – keeps their imaginations within bounds. As it happens, in my case the connotations I bring to the words are just those the adverbs seem to reinforce. Ramblers for me are energetic people in shorts and hiking boots, whereas those who meander are much less purposive. I imagine them in sandals with floppy hats on their heads. (Though not Mole, I hasten to add.)

Words carry emotional overtones

Frequently words are carefully chosen so that their connotations might conjure up an emotional response in the mind of the reader or listener, might persuade them to look at an issue from the writer's or the speaker's angle. In a recent edition of the *Today* programme on Radio 4, a speaker commented on criticisms of Tony Blair's welfare reforms: 'Anyone would think he was sending children back to the salt mines!' Presumably, he felt that this was such a patently absurd notion that to mention it would persuade everyone that the reforms were quite justifiable. In the same programme, the link between supermarkets and their suppliers was described as 'a master/slave relationship'. Before any words are written, or put into a prepared talk, a considerable amount of mental work takes place. The speaker or writer hopes to tap into shared experiences with the reader or listener, not just in terms of everyday life, but shared history, shared reading, films, TV programmes and so on. They can never be sure, of course, exactly what the effect of their words will be.

Figurative language

The description of the master/slave relationship mentioned above is just one example of how prevalent figurative language is in everyday life, although it's possibly something you have associated more with literature, especially poetry.[6]

One of the most interesting aspects of the passage from *The Wind in the Willows* is the words used to describe the river. It is seen by Mole as an animal, sleek, sinuous and full-bodied. To describe something as if it were something else, calling the supermarket's suppliers the slaves, or a river an animal, is to use a metaphor. If the writer had used a comparative word – if he had said that the river looked 'like' an animal, he would have been using a simile. These are types of what is known as figurative language. The connotations of the words used in the metaphors are interesting to consider. What kinds of associations are conjured up in your mind by the words 'sleek' and 'sinuous'?

Collocation; onomatopoeia; alliteration

Once we have been introduced to the idea of the river as an animal, we can look for other words that follow up the metaphor, that keep company with the 'animal' idea. Words that frequently go together are said to 'collocate'. Is the river a wild animal? A playful animal? A pet? All these ideas might collocate with 'animal' in the minds of most of us. Well, it seems too lively for a pet, but more 'boisterous' than 'wild'. It 'flings itself on fresh playmates', though they don't seem too concerned, shaking themselves free, but then being caught and held again. There is 'laughter', and synonyms for laughter, 'chuckling' and 'gurgling'. In building up the picture of the river, Kenneth Grahame uses a lot of onomatopoeic words. This term refers to words that actually suggest the sounds they represent: chuckling; gripping things with a gurgle; rustle and swirl; a-shake and a-shiver; chatter and bubble. Some of these words are alliterative. Alliteration is a term you are likely to have come across, meaning the repetition of a sound, usually the initial one, for a particular purpose or effect.

The sounds conjured up by the onomatopoeia and the alliteration are busy, energetic sounds, such as 'rustle' and 'swirl' not 'roar' or 'growl', so they add something to the kind of animal picture we were building earlier. I spoke in the last chapter of various kinds of grammatical cohesion, which help to give a unified feel to a text. We have here a good example of lexical cohesion, which has the same effect. The words I have picked out for comment, because they collocate happily with each other, make the piece hang together. We can build a picture of the river in our minds which makes sense to us.

Morphology

Another way of looking at this text at the word level would be to consider the structures of some of the words. The study of word structure is called morphology. A word's structure can be changed by adding letters to the beginning of the word (a prefix) or to the end (a suffix). Adding suffixes frequently changes the grammatical work a word does, and we have looked at some of these endings in the grammar chapter. If you have read that chapter, you might like to take a minute to consider whether there are any significant word endings you recognise in this passage before reading on.

One suffix you might have recognised was '-ing'. Kenneth Grahame mentions birds 'building', flowers 'budding' and leaves 'thrusting', and there are several more examples later on: 'chasing' and 'chuckling'; 'gripping' and 'leaving'. As I have several times pleaded in this book, do avoid the trap of playing games of 'spot the (in this case) -ing participle' with children. This is of no use at all unless you go on to discuss the effect the words have on the reader. And of course, while we can all be reasonably sure, after a while, of what an -ing participle is, the effect on the reader is much more open to interpretation. This is one of the most important lessons children can learn as they become more advanced readers, and you should go out of your way to encourage them to decide for themselves, after due consideration of the evidence, why the writer has made this grammatical choice. I'll refrain therefore from describing what the effect is on me, lest it should be taken by some readers as the definitive answer!

Morphemes

We have looked at two examples of suffixes in this passage, that is letters or groups of letters which can be added to the ends of words to change their grammatical function:

* '-ing' has been added to words like 'build' and 'bud' and 'thrust'.
* 's' has been added to words like 'glint' and 'gleam' and 'sparkle'.

This means that all these words now consist of two morphemes. Morphemes are, to quote David Crystal (1991, p.104), 'the smallest building blocks in the grammar of a language'. There are two kinds.

Free morphemes

The six words quoted above – 'build', 'bud' and so on – can stand alone or can be used as part of many other words: 'builder' or 'disbud' or 'gleamed', for example. In their original root form they are called free morphemes.

Bound morphemes

The other parts of the words, '-ing' and 's' and 'er' and 'dis' and 'ed', could not stand alone. They are called bound morphemes because they can only be found attached to free morphemes. Bound morphemes can be used to change the grammatical status of a word: 'er' changes 'build' from a verb to a noun, for example; 'ed' changes 'gleam' into a past tense. Bound morphemes can also be used to change the meaning of a word: 'dis' prefixed to 'bud' turns the word into something that means the opposite of the original.

Building our own word hoards

Before leaving the passage, I would like to return briefly to the question of increasing the reader's own vocabulary as a result of the experience of reading this text. A lot of the words in it are no longer current, even in fiction: words such as 'hither' and 'thither' or 'playmates' or 'a-shake and 'a-shiver'. These are a bit like museum pieces: interesting to look at, but not for current use. Some words, however, may be picked out by readers for further use. 'Meandered' is one that appeals to me, and that I might be tempted to try out when the opportunity arose. Whether it would stay active in my writing or speaking for long is another matter.

Building up one's personal word collection is rather like going for walks on a pebbly beach after the tide has gone out. There are lots of attractive stones lying around and we might be tempted to rush around picking them up. Yet very few will ever gain a permanent place on the shelf. Some will be dropped before leaving the beach, and even some of those which are taken home will lurk in the garage or a dark place in the garden, never really to be looked at again. Yet we will have enjoyed them all, however fleetingly, the colour, the texture, the feel of them. Children should be allowed to meet and enjoy words in a variety of contexts. Some they need not decode independently, or remember how to spell, for a long time after meeting them, if ever.

The attraction of unusual words

As I have implied in my comments about nursery rhymes, words can fascinate us and mesmerise us, even though we find them difficult to understand. Marcus, a teenage character in the novel *Still Life*, by A.S. Byatt (1985), starts to recover from the chronic depression he has been suffering through the unlikely agency of A-level botany. The author states that after months of not being able to involve himself in anything, he 'wrote quietly about the monoecious and dioecious households of trees and the extravagant mimetic capacities of the bee orchid'. She goes on to ask 'From where does the intense satisfaction come, that is to be taken in that kind of writing?' Or more simply, in listing and drawing as Marcus did:

Alopecurus – Fox-tail grass
Phalaris – Canary grass
Phleum – Cat's-tail grass …

The list goes on. What has a fascination for botanical terms got to do with primary children? An interest in jargon, in technical terms is not something that only comes in the secondary phase of schooling. The words in books like Stephen Biesty's, for example, will probably fascinate some Key Stage 2 readers far more powerfully than those in a story or poem ever will. Here, for example, is an extract from *Stephen Biesty's Incredible Everything* (1997) describing part of a Boeing 777:

The 777 is a 'fly-by-wire-' aircraft. Controls in the cockpit are not linked directly to the 'flight feathers' (control surfaces such as the ailerons, rudder and elevators). Instead, the pilot's sidestick sends signals to a computer system, which adjusts the aircraft's direction and altitude.

Even the very young reader can find technical terms fascinating. In stage one of Ginn's *All Aboard* reading scheme, beginner readers are introduced to a non-fiction book, *Honeybee*. On pages 6 and 7, we find a large drawing of the bee's three body parts, labelled 'head', 'thorax' and 'abdomen'. 'Pupae' and 'antennae' are also labelled on other pages, along with 'tongue', 'legs', 'wings' and 'eyes'. But while all these words may be savoured at the time of reading, they will not necessarily stay in the reader's mind for long.

Controlled vocabulary

This attitude to introducing specialised vocabulary in the earliest stages of reading represents a radical departure from that frequently mocked approach to beginning reading which took the same 12 words and used them over and over again: 'Here is Peter and here is Jane. Jane is here and Peter is here ...' and so on *ad nauseam*. This strange kind of text arose from too rigid an adherence to the notion of 'controlled vocabulary'. In the 'Look and Say' approach to reading, children were not required to break words down into their constituent sounds, but to remember them as wholes. New words were only introduced very gradually as the scheme progressed; they had a high rate of repetition and were carried over to following books in the series.

Key words

The Ladybird reading scheme, which featured Peter and Jane, was based on careful research into 'key words', the name given to a group of the most used words in the language (Murray 1969). The research established that a relatively few English words form a very high proportion of those in everyday use. It was calculated that 20,000 words form the vocabulary of an average adult, and of these, 12 key words make up a quarter of all the words we read and write. One hundred key words make up half of those in common use. It seemed very sensible, then, to build a set of early reading books on the basis of the gradual introduction of a few more key words each time, until children felt confident enough to read them. One unfortunate aspect of this approach is that the most frequently used words are, not surprisingly, 'bread and butter' words of no great colour or excitement. The first 12 consist of 'a', 'and', 'he', 'I', 'in', 'is', 'it', 'of', 'that', 'the', 'to' and 'was'. They have little or no colourful content, though they all play a vital role in the construction of sentences. They are an interesting set in a number of ways, not least because though 'he' is in the list, 'she' isn't!

Nowadays, though key words are still a feature of modern reading schemes, and lists of key words can be found in the National Literacy Strategy, writers of reading scheme material are urged to introduce them more naturally, alongside more exciting content words. The key words do need to be learned as quickly as possible, because they occur so frequently, but writers are free to introduce children to a wide variety of other words at the same time. Sometimes I find that students are still confused about the difference between these two categories of words, and avoid using a text with young children because it has some difficult words in it that beginner readers might not understand. These words, to return to my metaphor, are frequently the more colourful 'pebbles' that may be picked up very briefly and quickly discarded, but are likely to provide an interesting experience. Provided the text is being shared with a sensitive adult who knows what kinds of support to provide, they will not be offputting at all.

Children need to meet exciting words!

A point that I made in the grammar chapter holds true for words too. Children need to encounter writers who know how to be bold or innovative with words. In *Dinosaur Roar* (1996), a picture book by Paul and Henrietta Stickland, the verbs are 'roar', 'squeak', 'gobble', 'nibble', 'munch' and 'scrunch'. I would call this a bold bunch. The adjectives in the book are bold, too, and what is also helpful for young readers is that they help readers to see the dinosaurs in pairs of opposites, a concept that young children often find difficult to grasp. 'Dinosaur short', for example, can be compared with 'dinosaur very, very long' and 'dinosaur fat' with 'dinosaur tiny'.

Having fun with words

There are many texts where the chief aim is to have fun with words. A good example of this kind of text is *Don't Put Your Finger in the Jelly, Nelly*, by Nick Sharratt (1993). Photographs of various messy foods are very cleverly combined into illustrations of plates, bowls, paper bags, etc., and by means of a series of judiciously placed holes it is possible to create the illusion of poking one's finger into such things as a large jelly, a lemon meringue pie, a piece of cheese and a bowl of pasta. The fun comes when you turn over the page and find your finger is caught in the trunk of a 'jellyphant', or has been grabbed by a 'meringue-utan', or has woken up the 'spag-yeti'.

Invented words

A well-known example of invented words is Lewis Carroll's *Jabberwocky*:

* Twas brillig and the slithy toves
  Did gyre and gimble in the wabe;

All mimsy were the borogroves,
And the mome raths outgrabe.

Discussing this text provides a wonderful opportunity to compare the connotations the words have for each reader. We can't look the words up in a dictionary and so we are thrown back on associations, particularly associations with the sounds the words make – the onomatopoeic element of words which I referred to earlier. Lewis Carroll apparently formed 'brillig' by combining the two words 'boiling' and 'grilling' and had in mind a particular time of day when the evening meal was being cooked. To me, however, the words always suggest a description of the weather, and I can't rid myself of a picture of bright sunshine and stifling heat, with the slithy toves trying to keep cool by gyring and gimbling. (How many prefixes and suffixes can you attach to 'gyre' and 'gimble'? 'Disgyre'??? or 'Ungimble'??? What would they mean?)

Phonology[7]

Finally in this chapter, I want to say something about the smallest units of all of the English language – the sounds. Phonology is the name given to the study of the sound system of a language. A phonic strategy, when helping children to decode a word in a text, involves breaking the word down into its constituent sounds. This is not at all easy to do, especially for prereaders, who have largely experienced language as a continuous stream of sounds, where the word boundaries, let alone the sound boundaries, are very difficult to detect. Take for instance the child (he was in Key Stage 2) who wrote about the 'warmer morial'. He had never seen the words written down and had no clear idea of what they represented. When I taught in London, children used to write for me that they had been cycling up 'Blackifill' (Blackheath Hill) at the weekend. The difficulty is compounded here by the fact that the children spoke with a south London accent, which rendered /th/ as /f/.[8] Try to put yourself in the children's place by listening to a conversation between native speakers in a language you don't speak fluently. Can you detect the word boundaries?

Phonemes

When we come to the boundaries between the sounds, the difficulties are even greater. Pause for a moment and consider how many sounds you can hear in 'physical', 'frightened' or 'transport'. (You can check in the chapter notes if you are not sure.[9]) The human voice is capable of producing a very large range of sounds, especially if we take into account sounds produced with a rising note or with a falling note. In some languages, this difference in intonation is sufficient to signal a difference in meaning. Fortunately for me, as I have a poor ear for this sort of thing, this is not the case in English. In English, spoken that is with an RP accent (see p.55) there are 44 sounds that can cause a change of meaning. By this, I mean that when native speakers hear 'pin' and 'bin' clearly articulated, or 'cat' and 'cap' they will agree that two distinct objects have been referred to. These 44 basic units of sound are called phonemes. There are 20 vowel sounds, or phonemes, and 24 consonant sounds, or phonemes. It's not easy to write sounds down without having recourse to a phonetic alphabet, but examples of words containing these 44 sounds (highlighted in bold) are given below.

Vowel phonemes	Consonant phonemes
m**a**t	**b**all
r**a**ther	**ch**oose
r**are**	**d**aisy
p**aw**	**f**lower
s**ay**	**g**ate
p**e**t	**h**eat
m**ee**t	**j**am
f**ear**	**k**it**ch**en
f**ir**	**l**amb
l**i**d	**m**atter
p**ie**	**n**ote
h**o**t	cli**ng**
l**oa**n	**p**arcel
p**oo**l	**r**estaurant
f**oo**t	**s**un
m**ou**se	**sh**oes
oil	**t**omato
up	**th**ose
s**ure**	**th**ink
und**er**	**v**ase
	winter
	yacht
	zebra
	illu**s**ion

Figure 8.1 Phonemes of English

Allophones

You must remember, when listening to the words listed above that the sounds being represented are those that would be made by a speaker with an RP accent. Even these speakers will not all sound identical: such things as gaps in the teeth can affect the way the sounds are made. In addition, a sound such as /s/ will come out slightly differently depending on the other sounds around it. In pronouncing 'seat' the lips are spread, as if smiling. In 'soon', the lips are rounded. Yet a native speaker will probably be prepared to assert that the gap-toothed speaker, the one saying 'seat' and the one saying 'soon' are all pronouncing the same sound, or phoneme, /s/; the sounds are sufficiently close to come within the same 'segment' of sound in the sound continuum. These variants of /s/ are called allophones.

The sounds of English are differently distributed in other accents. In my native Lancashire for instance, the /oo/ sound in 'book' and 'cook' is the same as the /oo/ sound in 'moon' and 'look', so someone with a Lancashire accent saying 'Look at that cookery book', would make three identical /oo/ sounds in the sentence. The RP way of sounding the /oo/ in 'book' is used by speakers with a Lancashire accent in 'cup' and 'put'.

Syllables

To break a word into each of its constituent sounds is the most complex way of segmenting it. It is more straightforward to divide words into syllables. A syllable can be defined as the smallest unit of speech which normally occurs in isolation. There are a few vowels, such as 'I', which can exist by themselves, but more usually, a syllable consists of a combination of vowel and consonants, such as 'hat' or 'pen'. Another way of thinking about syllables is as 'beats' in the rhythm of a word. Children enjoy clapping out the syllables of their names. 'Anne' has one syllable, 'Mary' has two, 'William' has three and so on.

Onsets and rimes

Many groups of syllables share a similar pattern. Figure 8.2 gives examples.

p	en	s	at	t	ight
m	en	c	at	l	ight
h	en	fl	at	s	ight
t	en	m	at	m	ight

Figure 8.2 Syllable patterns

In these one syllable words, the letter or letters that come before the vowel are known as the onset. The rest of the syllable is called the rime. It is considered more helpful for beginner readers to be able to recognise patterns in rimes as in these examples than to launch into decoding a word like 'might' letter by letter. To say /m/ /i/ /g/ /h/ /t/, or 'tuh', as a child is likely to say, will not act as a useful prompt when decoding this word. If children can recognise 'ight' as a group of letters which occur in words such as 'sight' and 'fight' and 'might' and 'light', and can remember the sounds they make, they have aquired a useful decoding strategy. For further references to work on onset and rime see the chapter notes.[10]

Segmenting words

An experienced reader, when sharing a text with a beginner, must exercise judgement as to how to break the word up to be of most help – syllabically, by onset and rime, or phoneme by phoneme. Only for some of the time will this last option be the same as letter by letter. One of the great difficulties of reading and spelling English words is that though there are 44 sounds or phonemes, there are only 26 letters of the alphabet. It is obvious then that there can be no straightforward one to one correspondence between sounds and letters.

Graphemes

A grapheme is defined in the National Literacy Strategy as a 'written representation of a sound, which may consist of one or more letters'. You will find the word 'grapheme' differently defined in other sources, but that is the one I shall use here.

   Almost all the 44 English phonemes can be written down in a variety of ways. The sound /b/, for example, is written using one 'b' in 'ball', but in 'rabbit' two 'b's are used. The sound /f/ is written one way in 'flower', another in 'photograph' and differently again in 'enough'. /Sh/ in 'shoes' is different from /sh/ in 'sure'. The sound /k/ can be written as in 'queen' or 'kitten' or 'circus'. The sound we hear in 'pie' looks very different in 'I' and in 'knight'.

Graphs, digraphs, trigraphs

You will have noticed from the above examples that sometimes one letter of the alphabet is used to represent a sound. This is true of the sound /b/ in 'ball', and the sound /p/ in 'pie'. These written symbols are known as graphs. (Not to be confused with graphs in mathematics.) Sometimes, two letters of the alphabet combine to represent a sound. Two consonants combine to make the sound /sh/ in 'shine'. Two vowels, /ie/ combine to make the sound of the long /i/. This means that although there are only three sounds in 'shine', that is, /sh/ and /ie/ and /n/, there are five letters of the alphabet, because the letters 's' and 'h' combine to make what is called a consonant digraph, and the letters 'i' and 'e' combine to make a vowel digraph. Sometimes three letters of the alphabet, or even four, combine to make one sound. In the word 'knight', the long /i/ sound is represented by the letters 'i' and 'g' and 'h'. This is called a trigraph. This word has three sounds, but six letters, because as well as the trigraph, the sound /n/ at the beginning of the word is represented by a digraph, 'kn'.

The English spelling system

The complex correspondences between phonemes and graphemes add up to a very intricate spelling system. There are over 200 rules for combining letters of the alphabet to make the sounds of English. Traditional phonic approaches to reading oversimplify the system by telling children, in the early stages, that one letter makes one sound: 'a' is for 'apple', 'b' for 'ball', 'c' for 'cat'. Yet it must already be apparent to even four-year-old Amy that 'a' does not make that sound in her name. And how does Christopher account for the way he spells his? Experienced readers very rarely rely on phonic cues alone when deciphering a text, because they are the most complex cues of all. The National Literacy Strategies of England and Wales both stress a multistrategy approach to the teaching of reading, in which phonics plays an important part alongside other strategies. Phonics is frequently mentioned in the media as a reading strategy, but, in fact, a knowledge of phoneme/grapheme correspondences is far more likely to be needed when writing than when reading. Faced with a difficult word, no dictionary available and no one to ask, we may resort to trying to break the word down into sounds. This accounts for efforts like 'skool' or 'becos' in children's writing. No amount of listening to the sounds is ever going to reveal the presence of 'ch' or 'au' in these words. So in this instance too phonics is only of partial help, and we must learn to visualise words, rather than 'listen' to them. The more confident children become as readers and writers, using the full range of strategies available, the more we can hope to interest them in the vagaries of the English spelling system. Phonics investigations can play an interesting part in language work at Key Stage 2.

I know from experience that many students find phonology difficult. Yet words are such exciting things that I feel reluctant to leave this chapter with what you may have found to be a dull patch. I want to end therefore with this paean of praise to the word from George Keith and John Shuttleworth (1997, p.248):

> In dictionaries, words lie inert but the moment they are put to use they take on new dimensions. There is always something to say about a word once it is in action: its precise, denotative meaning; its connotations; its internal structure or morphology; its sound and rhythm; its appropriateness; its spelling. Even when it is not in use there are always its origins and subsequent history, its family connections, its spelling, its synonyms and antonyms, and statistical frequency to consider. Words are so multi-dimensional that more than one linguist has been driven to the simplest definition of all of words in writing: i.e., the bits between the spaces. In *A Mouthful of Air*, a very readable book about language, the novelist Anthony Burgess points out that it is only in the Western world that such a priority is given to grammar. In the East words are viewed as much more powerful and well able to take care of themselves.

Whichever way you look at it, the answer to the old question, 'What's in a word?' must be, 'Far more than the ear can hear and the eye can see'.

Chapter 9

Applying text, sentence and word level knowledge to fictional texts and poetry

In this chapter and the next, I want to show how the knowledge about language which I have been discussing in the last five chapters can be applied to exploring the meanings of texts which might be found in primary school classrooms.[1] I don't intend to produce materials for direct use in the classroom. There are many books available now which do this,[2] but they assume a degree of language awareness which not all students and teachers have available to them at the moment. Readers may therefore be condemned to following the suggestions on offer without a clear understanding of the underlying language knowledge or of how to adapt the ideas for use with other texts. My hope is to support teachers in building up their own language knowledge so that they will feel confident in selecting aspects of language work which will usually be text based, and planning a variety of interesting activities for their classes drawing on a wide range of texts.

Reading is meaning making

Before I embark on a discussion of any texts, can I remind my readers again of some points I made in Chapter 1. In reading any text, it is not enough to recognise and attach a label to the text structure the writer has chosen, or isolate examples of syntax or vocabulary for comment. In a book written for children, as in any other, we are primarily concerned with *making sense* of the text and the enjoyment and pleasure that doing this will give us. A good children's book may convey layers of meaning, some of them beyond those immediately accessible to very young readers. To make sense of such a book we draw on some general knowledge, but more particularly, we rely on what we as adults, know about interpreting texts. In the case of the texts in this chapter, we are drawing on our experience of what fiction and poetry has to offer to a reader who is sensitive to all the texts' possibilities for offering up meaning. Each of us may interpret what we read in a slightly different way, but our readings must be cohesive. That is to say they must be able to account in a reasonable way for all of the structures, the syntax and the words we have in front of us. In doing this, it is more than likely that we will draw heavily on shared knowledge and memories, and above all, on ways of reading that, if we have been fortunate, we have been taught ourselves and will try to pass on to children.

The Queen's Knickers, Nicholas Allen, Red Fox 1995

What kind of text is this?

This is a picture book, with words and pictures by the author, which addresses in a very amusing way the question of what the Queen wears underneath her smart coats and dresses. The text introduces us to a number of characters, including the Queen herself and Dilys the maid, who is in charge of the Queen's knickers. Though the book has characters, and it is obviously fictional, it is not a story. This is because there is no overall plot, there is no beginning, middle or end. Instead, the book falls into sections, which are described in the next paragraph. Some of the sections are 'mini-narratives'. Occasionally the word 'story' is still used in some classrooms, and by some publishers, as a generic term for almost any kind of reading or writing. In view of the number of text types which children are to be introduced to, and to be encouraged to create themselves, it's important to be precise in using the word.

In fact, this text purports to be a report on the subject, though of course a lot of the humour resides in the fact that there never would be any such document. Just to think of it smacks delightfully of lese-majesty. The 'report' characteristics begin immediately with the opening sentence. Instead of a past tense verb, telling of a specific event, which we would expect at the beginning of a story, the author uses a present tense, telling the reader the general state of things: 'The Queen likes to dress smartly'. As reports often do, the text falls into distinct sections.

- Section 1: shows us where the Queen keeps her clothes, in a large wardrobe, and where she keeps her knickers, in a slightly smaller chest of drawers. We meet Dilys the maid, and are told that one of her duties is to pack the knickers in a special trunk when the Queen goes away.
- Section 2: a short narrative section. We know it's narrative because it tells us of a specific event that happened 'one day'. The trunk went missing but happily was found again.
- Section 3: returns us to the reporting present tense. There are some pages of description of knickers for all eventualities.
- Section 4: we meet a new character, a little girl, and some first person writing of the 'what if' kind.

From then on, the text stays in this more personal mode, with the little girl wondering what knickers the Queen would wear if she visited her school. The blurb on the back of my Red Fox edition of the book suggests that 'Through the eyes of a little girl hoping for a school visit by the Queen, the range of royal underwear is revealed, in all its regal glory'. In fact, it seems to me that this misses the point that there is a sharp contrast between the pseudo 'official' tone of the first three sections, which provides the text with a lot of its humour, and the personal note that is struck at the end.

Sentence and word choices

The sentence structure and vocabulary of some sections of the text is reminiscent of a government document, though a simplified one. It is informative and neutral. One double page spread is actually labelled 'OFFICIAL H.M. KNICKER GUIDE'. The use of the acronym, the capitalisation and the page layout all reinforce the informative tone. Various pairs of knickers are illustrated and labelled. The connotations of the words on the captions imply some underlying knowledge of the royal family: corgis appear on a pair labelled 'At Home' for example, and a plaid pair has the label 'Balmoral (Woollen)'. Another acronym, VIP, also requires the reader to bring previous knowledge to bear in order to enjoy the joke. On this occasion, the letters refer to Very Important Pair. There are connotations too behind the reference to the Christmas knickers, which are 'a gift from Scandinavia'. Another source of humour in the text comes from a double page spread where there is a sharp contrast in types of vocabulary; on the first side we find a description of the Royal Knickers, which we are told are 'most valuable' and 'encrusted with diamonds, emeralds and rubies'. On the opposite side of the page, we find that they were first worn by Queen Victoria and are 'rather baggy'.

There is no grammatical cohesion linking the last, more personal section with what has gone before. The reader turns the page and encounters a girl sitting at her desk. She is not introduced – in fact, we never find out her name. All this leaves space in the text for the readers to create some links for themselves, to tell themselves what they recognise, and to speculate on what they would be thinking if they were in the girl's position. In contrast to the first part of the book, the words and pictures now take us 'behind the scenes at the palace' as the little girl imagines the Queen deciding on a new design to be worn on a royal visit to her school. The vocabulary becomes more colloquial: 'there'd be a *terrific* flap at the palace', 'too frilly ...', 'too silly ...', 'I shall just have to ...'. Of course, as I have already said, the fun resides in the fact that none of this could ever happen. The whole text is inviting children to 'think the unthinkable' and the grammatical structure reinforces this with the modal 'would' expressing something that 'might happen if ...': 'I wonder what knickers the Queen would wear ...' or 'I would tell her ...' or the elided form 'There'd be ...'.

Narrative interludes in the text

A personal story

The little girl's 'what if ...' story is narrated in the first person, and contains a lot of direct speech, set out in a conventional way, though only single speech marks are used to demarcate it. Publishers vary in their use of single or double speech marks and encouraging children to spot the different usages as they go from book to book is one way of drawing their attention to the use of direct speech in text. Another interesting aspect of direct speech is the variety of clues the writer gives to how these words might sound as they come out of people's mouths. This is particularly important if the text is to be read aloud with appropriate intonation and expression. Here, we have already been told that there is 'a flap' at the palace and both the Queen and Dilys look very put out. When the Royal Knickermaker is sent for, therefore, the exclamation marks which close each of the Queen's next utterances are a strong clue to Her Majesty's irritated tones. Capitalisation is used again, this time to indicate an even greater degree of royal irritation at the sight of what is considered a most unsuitable design. Another type of clue is employed when the writer tells us that the little girl 'whispered' to Her Majesty.

Environmental print

The book is full of indications to children of how texts of all kinds, captions, labels, posters and so on fulfil a useful purpose in every aspect of life. A nice example comes at the end of the little girl's story when she imagines a grateful monarch sending her a special note 'by the Royal Mail'. The language structure of the note is suitably lofty in tone: 'Her Majesty wishes to inform you ... most enjoyable ... very comfortable.'

A national crisis

To introduce the earlier narrative episode in the book, we have been told that Dilys, the maid, has a special trunk to transport the knickers when the Queen goes away. A dramatic note is introduced when the trunk goes missing. The language chosen to tell this story is much more official in tone: 'It caused a great crisis ...' This time, there is only a very small amount of direct speech, and instead another convention is used. The words 'The Queen's Knickers! The Queen's Knickers' are depicted coming out of Dilys's mouth, though there is no speech bubble or speech marks. With arms outstretched and mouth wide open, the picture of poor Dilys leaves us in no doubt at all about how these words are to be said. As we expect in narrative, the story is told in the past tense: 'One day, the trunk went missing ... It caused a great crisis...and was only just sorted out ...' Eventually we discover what had happened to the trunk. As I have just had to do in my text, (I wrote '*had* happened') the author then switches to a form of the past tense which enables him to depict events further back in time: 'The trunk *had got* mixed up with a picnic hamper'.

Reader involvement in the story

Because of the narrative strategies the author uses to tell the story of the trunk's disappearance, there are more opportunities for readers to join in and become 'text creators' themselves. These include:

- information presented in the illustrations rather than in the text
- a poster depicting the missing 'H.M.'S KNICKER TRUNK'
- police cars and helicopters, clearly labelled, shown rushing about
- a picture of a large television screen announcing 'NEWS AT TEN'.

There is more evidence of how useful labels are when we visit 'H.R.H. LAUNDRY' and find the puzzled laundry workers unpacking a chicken, bottles of wine and a tin labelled 'Biscuits'. On the washing line behind them, various items of clothing are all carefully labelled with the names of their royal owners.

Punctuation

Learning how to interpret textual conventions is an important part of becoming a reader. An important aspect of this learning concerns the role of punctuation in a text. Twice in *The Queen's Knickers* there are double page spreads with one line of text underneath each picture. The first example looks like this: 'So she has an enormous wardrobe for her clothes ...' (left-hand page) and 'and a slightly smaller chest of drawers for all her knickers' (right-hand page). A little further on, we find 'It caused a great crisis ...' followed by 'and was only *just* sorted out before it reached the NEWS AT TEN'. Traditional reading schemes tended to instil in children the idea that a line of writing was the same as a sentence. It's still not uncommon to find children letting their voices fall and coming to a halt at the right-hand margin, regardless of the punctuation or the sense. The dots are a clear indication here that more is coming and that the sense is not complete.

I have already mentioned that exclamation marks are helpful in indicating how words should be read aloud.

Brackets are used for an 'aside' or an 'Oh and by the way ...' type of comment.

Graphics

Italics are employed as an indicator of emphasis: examples are 'the trunk went *missing*!', 'was only *just* sorted out' and 'Don't worry about your knickers ... *no one can see them anyway*'.

Bold type is used to enhance the importance of the letter from the Queen, and there are various interesting examples of capitalisation throughout the book, providing prominent headings, or labels designed to be eye-catching.

In some of what I have said here, you will recognise parts of the text sentence and word level work in the National Literacy Strategy for Year 1 and Year 2 (all terms). Much of what I have said, goes beyond those particular objectives and no one would want to cover all these issues in one series of lesson plans. I have developed them in some detail in the hope that they will shed more light on some of the points I was making in earlier chapters.

Owl Babies, Martin Waddell, illustrated by Patrick Benson, Walker Books 1992

What kind of text is this?

This text has a classic story structure. It begins by introducing the characters, three baby owls, and we meet them at a specific time and a particular place in their lives. It's usual to be given extra information about the characters in a story, and in this case we learn their names, Sarah and Percy and Bill. This puts the story within a long tradition of anthropomorphised animal stories for children. They are actually 'semi-anthropomorphised': by this I mean that they have some human characteristics. They have names and they talk to each other, exploring their feelings, and we are told that they think a lot. But they don't wear clothes, drive cars or go for picnics, in the way that the more fully anthropomorphised animals in texts such as *The Wind in the Willows* do.

The time is 'Once' and the setting for their story is their house. We have extra information about this too. It's 'a hole in the trunk of a tree' and it has twigs and leaves and owl feathers in it. The illustration on this first page provides the reader with a very close perspective on the owls, so close indeed that readers might feel as if they are peeping into the hole. It is quite obviously night time and very dark. Even before this page is reached, the book's intriguing end papers have provided the reader with what could be regarded as a very detailed, owls' eye view of the tree, or possibly, if the page is held at arm's length, the patterns could be said to depict an owl with its eyes tight shut. This uncertainty in interpreting the design reminds readers of how similar owls and tree trunks are in colour and markings.

Narrative perspective

The owls live in the tree with the person they call 'Mummy', but who the writer refers to as their 'Owl Mother'. The story is narrated by the author in the third person: we are looking at and listening to the owls. The story is being told about them, not by them. This is emphasised on the second page, when Martin Waddell uses the phrase 'Owl Mother' again: 'One night, they woke up and their Owl Mother was GONE.' After this, we hear each of the baby owls talking about their 'mummy' until 'their Owl Mother' returns on the last page. You might like to consider the connotations you bring to the words 'Owl Mother'. They seem to me to hint at an archetypal mother/child relationship, seen from the readers' perspective, though to Sarah, Percy and Bill she is just *their* mummy. When the word is used as a title, it has a capital 'M' as in, 'Where's Mummy?' This is because here it is functioning as a proper noun. When it is referring to one of the group of people who are mothers, it has a lower case 'm' ('"I want my mummy," said Bill') because it is being used as a common noun. Other nouns that can belong in both classes are president, queen, princess: 'The president is the head of state', but 'The building was inaugurated by President Clinton'.

Plot structure

Once the characters have been introduced and their setting established, the main problem which the story explores is, interestingly, a psychological one: the baby owls' fear of being left alone in the dark. There are no villains in this story, nothing comes to threaten the owls, and as I hinted in the last paragraph, they are actually very much at home in their habitat and well camouflaged. Nature has equipped owls to be most at home in the dark. But, the author suggests, as yet they don't *feel* safe, for exactly the same reasons as many of the child readers of this story. The night seems very black, and very big, and full of movement. The illustrations are extremely successful in depicting the owls' feelings of vulnerability. Patrick Benson manages to convey an amazing variety of expressions on owl faces.

Characters

To study the characters is frequently one of the main pleasures of reading a story, and it is particularly important in this story because of the absence of events. Everything hinges around how each of the owls copes with the situations they find themselves in. Writers have a variety of means of depicting character. Readers are sometimes told about them directly, by the author, or can form judgements about them from what other characters say. What they do is also very revealing. More than anything in this story, it is what they say, the words that the writer puts into their mouths, which reveal their personalities. A pattern is established whereby almost always, when one speaks, all the owls speak, always in the same order, oldest to youngest. This makes them seem 'an entity', they are the 'owl babies'. Interestingly, the title of the book has no definite article: *Owl Babies* hints at the generic, rather than the specific, in the same way that I suggested 'Owl Mother' seemed to represent a type, rather than a particular one.

Sometimes writers will go to some lengths to find variants of 'said'. In this text, apart from setting the ball rolling with '"Where's Mummy," asked Sarah', almost all the other examples of direct speech are followed by 'said'. This has the effect of emphasising the fact that they spoke 'as members of a team', and also perhaps that they were feeling very subdued.

Sarah's role, as befits the eldest, is to draw attention to the problem in the first place, then to suggest possible reasons for it, and to offer comfort to the others, and hope. When hope seems dead, she's the first to voice their fears. Percy, who has that difficult position in any family, the middle child, largely reacts to what

Sarah says, and Bill, the baby, says the same thing throughout: 'I want my mummy.' In trying to offer comfort, Sarah suggests 'She'll bring us mice and things that are nice'. The rhyme here, and the word order, are strongly reminiscent of lines from a nursery rhyme, such as 'Sugar and spice, and all things nice ...'. The unspoken assumption is that Sarah is valiantly trying to 'play mummy' at this point and to remind her brothers of something they have shared with their mother. She is only partially successful, as the choice of words for Percy's rejoinder, 'I suppose so!', makes clear. Interestingly, the one occasion when Percy seems to be more than just an echo of Sarah is when, for the first time, she voices her fears: 'Suppose she got lost.' This seems to free him to say what's on his mind too and his idea is even more dramatic than Sarah's – a fox might have got her. This all seems so dreadful that the baby owls 'shut down all systems', close their eyes and just endure. And at this point, their mother returns, coming from behind them, so that we have a back view of them too, enduring on their branch. Alliteration heightens the effect: 'Soft and silent, she swooped through the trees .... It's interesting to consider your response to these words. In other contexts, we might have interpreted the words with their repeated 's' sounds, as sinister or threatening, yet here we read them as expressions of motherly love.

When the baby owls see her, the unvaried repetitions of 'said' are abandoned: '"Mummy," they cried.' This is the time to switch to action, and the verbs are of the bold variety I have referred to in an earlier chapter. They 'flapped' and they 'danced' and they 'bounced'. Their mother is not given very many words, but what she says is a very typically 'motherly' thing: 'WHAT'S ALL THE FUSS? ... You knew I'd come back.'

Some characteristics of speech

A close look at the words that come out of the mouths of the baby owls reminds the reader that people frequently don't speak in complete sentences. Often, they complete a previous speaker's sentences, as Percy does, when, after Sarah has said, 'I think she's gone hunting', he adds 'To get us our food!'. Or they add a comment of their own to what a previous speaker has said. Here is Percy again, this time adding to Sarah's 'She'll be back' his comment, 'Back soon!'. Sentences frequently begin with 'and' or 'but', including one of the most important sentences in the whole book, so important that it is written on a page by itself, in capital letters: 'AND SHE CAME'. Beginning sentences with 'and' and 'but' is an issue of usage, rather than of grammar. Interestingly, I have found that people who claim to be totally ignorant of grammar are still very much exercised by these 'rules of usage'. They seem to remember nothing from school about nouns, verbs, subordinate clauses and so on, but branded on their memory are rules of usage, such as these, or the one about never splitting an infinitive (as in *Star Trek*'s opening sequence mentioning: 'To boldly go ...'). David Crystal (1991) tells a story of how once, on a radio programme, he got a letter which said, 'Children who split infinitives are much more likely to go around breaking shop windows'. You may well have strong views of your own on this subject, but you need to be aware that you will find 'ands' and 'buts' starting sentences in some of the most beautiful prose and poetry in English. And, increasingly, you will find split infinitives too.

Punctuation

As in *The Queen's Knickers* a sentence in a bracket is used for an aside: '(all owls think a lot.)' It's a comment that is repeated several times throughout the book, so it's hard to ignore. It reminds readers of the place owls have in our culture and mythology, as symbols of wisdom, the emblem of Athena, goddess of Wisdom.

Speech marks in this text are of the double variety.

Exclamation marks are frequently used to reinforce the owls' feelings of fear and dismay, and as in *The Queen's Knickers* words in italics also heighten these feelings or add emphasis: '"I think we should *all* sit on *my* branch," said Sarah'. One of the most vivid uses of italics is in the sentence 'It was dark in the wood and they had to be brave, for things *moved* all around them'. This sinister sentence is brilliantly supported by the illustration, which shows a very large, dark wood and three very tiny owls. Our perspective as readers is from some distance away, in the wood. However closely we look, we can see nothing that might be moving other than leaves or grasses. But if we stop and think about this, and allow ourselves to empathise with the owls, we may remember how sinister the rustling of leaves and grass can sound in the dark. This is another example of sparseness of text working more dramatically than too much writing. Readers are well able to supply some ideas for themselves, thus drawing them in to the story.

The Queen's Knickers is an amusing text, working entirely on a surface level. We may enjoy going back to it again and again, but we are very unlikely to read any more into it on subsequent rereadings. It is none the worse for that. *Owl Babies* on the other hand is one of those books that, though written with children in mind, will continue to have significance for its readers long after they have conquered their fear of the dark.

The Frozen Man, Kit Wright, in *A Year Full of Poems*, edited by Michael Harrison and Christopher Stuart-Clark, Oxford University Press 1991

What kind of text is this?

Because of the layout, the text works visually as well as verbally to create an image of a winding path on the page. Much of the poem's drama comes from the contrast the poet establishes between two settings, one hostile, one welcoming.

The Frozen Man
Kit Wright

Out at the edge of town
where black trees
crack their fingers
in the icy wind
and hedges freeze
on their shadows
and the breath of cattle,
still as boulders
hangs in rags
under the rolling moon,
a man is walking
alone:
on the coal-black road
his cold
feet
ring
and
ring.
Here in a snug house
at the heart of town
the fire is burning
red and yellow and gold:
you can hear the warmth
like a sleeping cat
breathe softly
in every room.
When the frozen man
comes to the door,
let him in,
let him in,
let him in.

Figure 9.1

The 'frozen man' of the title is making his way from one to the other. Apart from the title, where the word 'frozen' arouses images in the mind of the reader of extreme cold, or even of somebody in whom life is temporarily suspended, we are told no more about the man until the setting he is travelling through has been well established. It's a cold and lonely one. There are no signs of human habitation, and very little movement of any kind on the ground except the stiff crackling of frozen branches in the wind. In contrast to this darkness and stillness, the moon rolls overhead. The man is alone. The text layout chosen by the poet enables him to put the word on a line by itself, which gives it extra significance.

The man seems to be pushing along at a fairly rapid rate, because his footsteps ring on the road. The short lines too seem to suggest quick movement. In today's world particularly, a man walking along a lonely road at night could suggest to some readers that he is up to no good. But as we read on, the evidence suggests that there is no danger here. The poet carefully places the readers, with himself, 'Here', in the much more friendly setting of a warm house in the heart of town. We are told that we can 'hear' the warmth – an unusual word to choose perhaps, but this is a live fire, burning in the hearth. This is the very house that the frozen man is aiming for. We realise that he represents no threat when we reach the last three lines of the poem: the imperative is used not just once but three times, to urge strongly the readers to let him in. The mystery remains of who is the owner of the house, who the lonely man is and what the connection between them. It's made very clear by the poet that the heart of town is the place to be on such a night. The countryside in contrast is cold an unwelcoming. This reverses images which are frequently presented in stories and poems of the hot and dusty town as a place to escape from into the fresh air of woods and fields.

Sentences

The poem consists of three sentences: one is used to establish the scene in the countryside, one in the town and the third to give the order to let the man in. The first two are deliberately contrasted with parallel words to open each sentence: 'Out at the edge of town', and 'Here … at the heart of town'. In the first sentence, the hostile environment is established in a series of relative clauses which accumulate in the readers' minds to create a picture of something a person would want to move briskly through and out of. There are three of these clauses:

- where black trees crack their fingers in the icy wind
- hedges freeze on their shadows
- the breath of cattle, still as boulders, hangs in rags under the rolling moon.

The sense of these images piling up one on top of the other is reinforced by the use of 'and' to link each one of them to the one that has gone before. Grammatically, one of these 'ands' is redundant, but would the description of the night's conditions be the same without it? There is a similar use of 'and' for emphasis, especially as the word gets a line to itself, in

his cold
feet
ring
and
ring.

There's a less hurried tone in the second sentence. No one is hurrying away from the warmth and glow of the fire. The sentence is constructed in such a way that emphasis falls heavily on the main clause:

- the fire is burning red and yellow and gold.

Punctuation

Both this sentence and the first one make use of colons (:). Colons have an anticipatory effect. They lead the reader on from what precedes to what follows. They seem to be very suitable punctuation marks therefore in the context of this poem. Colons can have several uses. In both cases in this text they seem to point to the relationship between one clause to another; they keep us moving along the road, as it were, without the halt that a full stop would bring about. When the full stop does come therefore, after 'room', as we wait for the frozen man to arrive and knock on the door, the stronger pause seems all the more dramatic.

Word choice

The meanings I have been suggesting at text and sentence level seem to be reinforced at the word level. The sounds of words are frequently important in reinforcing their sense. In the cold first half of the poem, we find the internal rhyme of 'black' with 'crack', cold, hard sounds. In the second half, the sounds are of the murmuring and hissing of the fire: 'warmth' and 'breathe', 'sleeping and softly'. Colours too provide strong contrasts: 'black', 'shadows' and 'coal-black' contrasting with 'red' and 'yellow' and 'gold'.

Figurative language

There is a ghostly, other-worldly feeling about the countryside. This comes partly from the author's treatment of the trees: they are personified, cracking their fingers in the icy wind. The cattle's breath adds to the ghostly effect, hanging in rags, while the cattle themselves seem more dead than alive, standing still as boulders. Over all this, we imagine the moon casting an unearthly light. The words used to describe the house all have living, breathing connotations. The house is at the 'heart' of town, for example. Consider the possible synonyms for this word, and what their effects might have been. The centre of town? The middle of town? The idea of the heartbeat is picked up by the description of the warmth from the fire which can be heard breathing softly. The simile used is 'like a sleeping cat', a reference which usually carries overtones of peaceful domesticity. The house is 'snug', a word which has strong connotations of warmth and cosiness.

Each reader will bring different images to this scene. It can be understood on a literal level, as someone coming home after travelling, or after work perhaps. On the other hand, it is possible to see the whole poem as an extended metaphor, a plea for forgiveness perhaps, from someone who has been 'out in the cold'. Reading, let me say again, is a matter of personal interpretation of the evidence in the text. This particular text allows for some freedom of interpretation.

Harry Potter and the Philosopher's Stone, J.K. Rowling, Bloomsbury 1997

What kind of text is this?

The novel is largely set in a fantasy world which exists alongside the world most of us live in, but in another dimension. It helps to appreciate its humour if readers can bring to it experience of reading other kinds of narrative texts, especially traditional school stories of the 'Jennings' variety. This is because many of the features of a boarding school story are to be found here, but humorously adapted to a magical dimension. For example, Harry Potter goes off to Hogwarts School for Wizards on the school train, which leaves Kings Cross from Platform 9¾. He has spent some time in London, getting his school uniform and his kit together, but these consist of items such as: three sets of plain work robes (black); one plain pointed hat (black) for day wear; one pair of protective gloves (dragon hide or similar); one wand; one cauldron (pewter, standard size 2). The exotic details and the mundane sit amusingly side by side. New pupils are told, for example, that 'all pupils' clothes should carry name tags'. There are bossy prefects and nervous first years on the school train. There are school rules: pupils may have pets, but they must be owls or cats or toads. No first years are allowed their own broomsticks.

Creating an imaginary world

We can accept this imaginary world because it is presented to us with a convincing completeness. It has a social and political order. For example, there is a Ministry for Magic whose job it is to make sure that Muggles, which is the name given to non-wizards, never find out about the magical dimension. It has a history, and a flora and fauna. We know something about these from the titles of the books Harry has to have for school, and from the books in the school library. They have titles like *A History of Magic* by Bathilda Bagshot and *One Thousand Magical Herbs and Fungi* by Phyllida Spore. It has a bank – Gringotts – run by goblins, with vaults which go deep under London, and its own monetary system.

The central character

It's not just memories of school stories that come to mind when reading this book. The plot provides powerful resonances of many other kinds of text. As in so much children's fiction, Harry Potter is an orphan. His parents have been killed by the arch villain, Voldemort, who is still around and very much a threat to Harry himself. Harry is brought up by a Muggle aunt and uncle, who treat him cruelly and try to prevent him finding out that he is a wizard. Readers know about Harry's latent powers, though he is kept in ignorance, and therefore wait with interest to see how he will be rescued from his miserable Muggle existence.

At Hogwarts School for Wizards, though he knows by now that he has an important destiny, Harry feels weak and threatened by both bullying pupils and powerful professors, one of whom at least appears to hate him. As in many a good fairy story, however, when he meets the many tribulations that come his way, he is given powerful aids: faithful friends, a 'cloak of invisibility' and, best of all, because he turns out to be good at Quidditch, the school game, he acquires a powerful broomstick, a 'Nimbus 2000'.

His final encounters with the powers of evil are reminiscent of legend or of Greek mythology. He first meets his enemies in an enchanted forest but doesn't recognise them for what they are. He is helped on that occasion by centaurs, who live in the forest. The climax of the struggle comes after a series of trials reminiscent of the labours of Hercules, deep in the underground labyrinthine cellars of the school. One of the memorable things about the text is the way it can switch from tongue in cheek humour like the spectacle of a dragon's egg hatching to the gruesomeness of the arch villain, Voldemort, drinking the blood of a dead unicorn.

The importance of names

The characters include the Dursleys, Harry's aunt, uncle and cousin, who are the most Muggle of all Muggles, Albus Dumbledore, the head at Hogwarts, and among Harry's school friends, the swot Hermione, the school bully, Malfoy, and his henchmen, Crabbe and Goyle. There is a taciturn school caretaker called Filch, Hagrid the faithful retainer with a rather murky past and, of course, the evil Voldemort himself. The author is clearly very much alive to the power of names. The names are redolent with the characteristics of those who own them. It's not surprising therefore that she makes 'Voldemort' a name that only the truly brave can bring themselves to utter: to others he is known as 'You-Know-Who'.

Settings

The prosaic and the magical also sit side by side in the descriptions of the settings too. For example, the train ride to Hogwarts could have been straight out of any school story, though with some interesting additions. Yet the first sight of the school is from another genre altogether. The pupils walk down a steep, narrow path and arrive at the edge of a great black lake. They round a bend and 'Perched atop a high mountain on the other side, its windows sparkling in the starry sky, was a vast castle with many turrets and towers'. They are ordered into a fleet of little boats and 'moved off all at once, gliding across the lake which was as smooth as glass'. These are words and images from a story of King Arthur, and yet a few seconds later Hagrid is shouting 'Heads down!' and 'Oy, you there! Is this your toad?' before returning readers to the magical by knocking three times on the castle door.

Issues at word level

Homophones

A lot of the richness of this book is at the text and the word level. The name J.K.Rowling chooses for ordinary, non-magical mortals, 'Muggles' is possibly a homophone for 'Muddles'. Homophones are words which sound the same but have a different meaning or a different spelling. More mundane examples include 'tale' and 'tail' or 'bred' and 'bread'.

Playing with words

I have referred to the fairy tale nuances of the text: one aspect of this is a magic mirror, known as 'The Mirror of Erised'. The name is a mirror image of 'desire'. The mirror shows those who look into it what they most desire.

The emotional impact of sounds

The phonology, or sound system of English is exploited, often in the names chosen for characters or places. Sounds are not neutral: those hearing them associate them with particular qualities and attributes, as I described when discussing accents in Chapter 6 (p.56). Hogwarts School has four houses, and their names immediately convey to native English speakers something of the qualities of each house: they are Hufflepuff, Ravenclaw, Slytherin and Gryffindor. Could Harry, the noble hero of this tale, have been in Hufflepuff? It seems unthinkable. As these word associations are an important part of the way meaning is made in this book, one wonders how differently the text is read in America, where it has had great success though under a different title, *Harry Potter and The Sorcerer's Stone*. In an interview for an American magazine, Joanne Rowling says that she enjoyed editing the book for the American version: 'The differences between "British English" (of which there must be at least 200 versions) and "American English" (ditto!) are a source of constant interest and amusement to me'.

The book is too long and too full of language richness to discuss it all in detail, but I would like to take one episode to look at more closely to give some indication of aspects that might be explored as part of some planned literacy hour work.

A closer look at one episode at text, sentence and word level

Text

The extract I have chosen is in Chapter 10. Harry Potter has shown remarkable prowess on a broomstick, and so against all the Hogwarts traditions he has been chosen to play Quidditch for his house, Gryffindor. He has no knowledge of the game at all and so is to be given some private coaching by Wood, the house Quidditch captain. One of the difficulties for authors of inventing worlds is that readers can inevitably bring no previous experience of any kind to bear in reacting to them. The author has to work hard therefore to build belief. If the game in question was rugby, or croquet, it would bring with it lots of associations, though not necessarily the same ones of course for all readers. Quidditch, we are told, has a long and honourable history. We know this because books have been written about it, such as *Quidditch Through the Ages*, and traditions have grown up around it, such as that first years don't usually play. We know that it is a great honour to play for the house. In this way, the author links our ideas of the game to what we might know about rugby, lacrosse or other sports with a long school tradition.

Figurative language

Another difficulty is that no reader will have the slightest idea of how to play the game, and yet it is important for the plot that some of the rules at least are understood. One way of explaining how to play would be to compare the game with something else. Yet again, in an invented world, similes and comparisons of all kinds can be difficult. How can characters who don't live in the 'real' world make such comparisons, or understand them? The author is helped here by the fact that Harry Potter was brought up as a Muggle, though Wood was not. She is able therefore legitimately to put a comparison into Harry's mind. She tells us that 'At either end of the pitch were three golden poles with hoops on the end. They reminded Harry of the little plastic sticks Muggle children blew bubbles through, except that these were fifty feet high'. Later on though, when Harry tries to use basketball as a simile for Quidditch, 'That's sort of like basketball on broomsticks with six hoops'. Wood doesn't understand, and Harry quickly drops the point (though the readers will have been enlightened by the comparison).

Sentences

We are also helped to learn the rules of Quidditch because Harry himself is very ignorant, but very keen to learn. The author has him hanging on to Wood's every word, and repeating everything Wood tells him, which gives readers ample opportunity to learn alongside him. Wood is also trying to make his speech as clear as he possibly can as befits someone who is trying to teach the rules of a game to a beginner.

'This ball's called the Quaffle,' said Wood. 'The Chasers throw the Quaffle to each other and try to get it through one of the hoops to score a goal. Ten points every time the Quaffle goes through one of the hoops. Follow me?'

'The Chasers throw the Quaffle and put it through the hoops to score', Harry recited.

Words

There are lots of invented words for readers to remember, such as 'Quaffle', 'Bludgers' and 'Snitch'. One's tempted on first reading the passage, to wonder whether the author couldn't have done better here. The words really do sound rather stupid. And then one remembers the words of Il Duce to his son-in-law in *Captain Corelli's Mandolin* by Louis de Bernières: 'Been playing golf? I thought so … I wish I had time for it myself. One feels so much at sea when talk turns to mashie-niblicks, cleeks and mid-irons.'

Though there's a lot to remember, there are sufficient similarities with more traditional games to prevent readers feeling totally lost. And then just when we feel on fairly familiar ground, the writer throws in a totally outrageous point: 'A game of Quidditch only ends when the Snitch is caught, so it can go on for ages – I think the record is three months, so they had to keep bringing on substitutes so the players could get some sleep.'

The comments I have made on these four books arise of course from my own readings of them. By now, you should be sufficiently familiar with what I have been saying about the processes of reading not to be surprised if your reading of these texts is different from mine. I hope that I have grounded my readings sufficiently in the linguistic evidence I had in front of me, but my *understanding* of that evidence, the meanings and hence the enjoyment that I take from each text, are to a large extent a matter of my own history as a reader and as a native English speaker.

Chapter 10

Applying text, sentence and word level knowledge to non-fiction texts

Splish Splash Splosh! A Book about Water, Mick Manning and Brita Grandstrom, Franklin Watts 1997

What kind of text is this?

This is an 'explanation' type of text, giving an account of the processes involved in the water cycle, but constructed in such a way as to make the information very accessible and interesting for Key Stage 1 readers. This is partly achieved because of the illustrations which form half of each double page spread. A small boy and his dog are shown taking part themselves in each stage of the cycle. Sometimes, as when, for example, the writers start the account on the beach, or when the water reaches the stage of being piped into and out of homes, the boy and his dog are seen against a background of everyday life going on around them. At other times, as they are whisked out into the deep ocean on a dolphin's back, or sail high in the sky on a cloud, they have left the everyday world of mothers, sisters, shopping and other mundane occupations far behind them. Because it is an explanation of a process, as water is sucked from the sea only to return to it eventually as rain, it makes sense to read the book from the beginning. There is no index or contents page, encouraging readers to jump in at an intermediate point, though there is a glossary with page references.

This book is ideal for sharing with an adult or more experienced reader, because there is so much to talk about in the illustrations, in the text itself and the diagrams that support and reinforce the words.

The structure of the text

It is usual for an explanation text to open with a general statement to introduce the topic, and then for each statement to be linked in a series of logical steps, perhaps using sequencing words such as 'next' or 'then'. Instead, each double page spread starts with the words:

• Splish, Splash, Splosh.

This enables even an inexperienced reader to join in the reading and have some fun. The sounds of the words are a constant reminder that it is water that we are thinking about. The writers are in no hurry to get on to a 'next' or 'then' stage. Readers are free to take the explanations at their own pace and are encouraged to daydream and to wonder as well as to learn.

As the text starts, we find ourselves on the beach with the boy and his dog. There is no introductory statement. Instead, after reminding readers of what they have observed waves doing on the beach, they are faced with the question which is to be pursued through the rest of the book: 'Where do they come from and where do they go?'

We are shown scenes we are probably familiar with – waves coming gently and gracefully into shore, slapping against boats and jetties – and then, as the boy sweeps out to sea on the dolphin's back, we sail off into the more unfamiliar and exotic parts of the water cycle. The facts are conveyed in memorable word pictures.

• We find out, for example, that parts of the sea are so deep that huge mountain ranges can lie under the surface.
• We are encouraged to envisage sea water splashing over dolphins' backs and between sharks' teeth.
• On another occasion, when the water cycle reaches the sewage stage, we discover how bath water mixes with other waste water and runs along sewer tunnels, and we are shown a cut away view of a typical high street. While shoppers go about their business, not very far beneath their feet rats and an alligator paddle in the sewer and we learn that unwanted pets are found there having been flushed down the toilet!

The writers' stance towards the readers

Initially, the writers adopt an impersonal, informative tone, but as the text reaches the domestic water stages they address the readers directly, reminding them that they are part of the process and have a role in ensuring that nothing goes wrong with it: 'Then it joins the mains water supply to your house! ... You have a wash ...', and finally, 'We have to be very careful and keep water clean ...'

Graphic conventions

The text is laid out in interesting ways, with one typeface for the stages of the water cycle and another for incidental but related pieces of information. Sometimes text is laid across a page in waves or following the contours of a rainbow. Diagrams are clearly labelled and provide a valuable support to the text.

Sentence structure

In one or two places, I think the syntactic pattern chosen might confuse inexperienced readers. Subjects of sentences have been in the plural:

- waves
- clouds
- raindrops
- streams

then the sentence pattern changes:

- Streams rush headlong into a crazy waterfall, that crashes into a river ... and fills up a dam.

Then we are given more information about 'the' dam. To the experienced reader, this use of the singular represents waterfalls, rivers and dams *in general*. To a young reader, the impression might well be given that there is only one of each.

Word choices

The vocabulary helps considerably to make the text appealing to younger readers. The words chosen are more colourful than those usually employed to describe a scientific process. Sometimes they have an onomatopoeic quality:

- waves 'slop' under boats, and 'slap' against harbours and jetties
- sea water 'washes' over dolphins' backs, and 'slips' through shipwrecks.

Almost all the verbs attract the readers attention:

- waves 'come roaring in'
- raindrops 'burst from the clouds'
- clouds 'swirl into a storm'
- monsoons can 'destroy buildings and flood towns'.

Adjectives too are vivid: rainwater is 'wild' and 'muddy'. In the sewers, waste water becomes 'thick and sludgy'.

Figurative language

Both similes and metaphors are found in the text. We are told that waves 'dance', waterfalls are 'crazy' and water 'splutters'. Clouds come sailing inland, like ships.

Technical terms

In spite of the quite poetic quality of the writing, there is plenty of information available and readers are introduced to terms such as 'chlorine', 'reservoir', 'evaporation', 'filter' and 'U-bend', in addition to the ones I have already mentioned.

It isn't easy to present accurate scientific information in such a way as to hold the interest and attention of young, inexperienced readers. In this book, words, pictures and diagrams work together admirably in an original mixture to achieve this. It would be interesting to discuss both this text and the next one I shall discuss, even with readers at Key Stage 2, as fascinating examples of the different ways in which it is possible to construct non-fiction texts.

Spider Watching, **Vivian French, illustrated by Alison Wisenfeld, Walker Books 1994**

What kind of text is this?

The blurb on the front and back covers of this book gives an inkling of one aspect of the writer's intention: to persuade readers to overcome any prejudice they may have towards spiders. 'Learn to love spiders', readers are urged, and 'cousin Helen hated spiders – until she looked more closely at their webs and saw what clever, interesting creatures they are …'.

Text structure

The book is structured ingeniously to achieve its aim of showing children that spiders are harmless, interesting and, in this country at least, nothing to be afraid of. The right-hand side of each double page spread consists of a narrative, the left-hand page provides the scientific information. Thus the emotional appeal of a story can be reinforced by revelations from natural history.

Narrative sections: plot and characters

On the narrative side, though the plot is simple, the story is effective. This is no crude use of narrative simply to 'sugar the scientific pill'. The action revolves around the writer's memory of a childhood visit made by her cousin, Helen. The story is told by Vivian French in the first person. Helen hated spiders, whereas the author and her brother were very fond of them. As the story goes on, Helen's feelings and attitudes change and develop. We have evidence for this from the things she does, and from what she says. For example, she is prepared to handle a spider, and pleads with the children's mother not to sweep all the spiders out of the shed.

This change of heart is really no thanks to the author's brother, who is cast in the role of 'technical expert'. He puts Helen right in a rather superior way whenever she exaggerates or makes inaccurate statements. We are told by his sister that this was 'part of his character'. She says, 'My brother liked people to get things right'. He is keen on telling his cousin all the gory bits of information, and pushes her to take the next step before she is quite ready for it.

The author herself comes across clearly as a more diplomatic character. She seems to be looking for ways of starting the change process in her cousin, beginning by drawing Helen's attention to the beauty of a web. Helen feels guilty when she accidentally damages it and takes her first step towards admiring spiders instead of fearing them when she sees how the web is mended. Vivian French seems to sense that a significant step has been made, and takes everyone off for breakfast. The next move is to offer to show Helen a web, and again she is overcome with guilt when it is discovered that the children's mother is about to placate her guest by sweeping all the spiders out of the shed. Helen becomes a 'spider defender' and from there, swiftly, a spider lover. Plot and characters then, two of the staples of story structure, have been handled in a subtle way in a relatively short space. No criticism has been made of Helen though her fear has been shown to be unnecessary. The point has also been made that the subject of spiders has enough in it to interest all kinds of people – the gentle and the more bloodthirsty.

Structuring the information

The non-narrative text is skilfully linked to the story. As we become involved in the feelings of each of the three main characters, issues are thrown up which are explored on each parallel page.

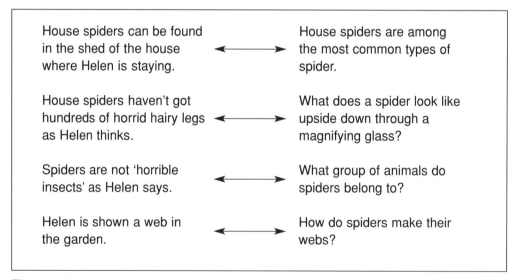

Figure 10.1

This does mean of course that the more piecemeal approach which I characterised in Chapter 5 as being typical of reading non-fiction is not appropriate here. It is not the readers' questions which are being addressed so much as

Helen's, and so the facts are read in the order which the narrative determines. An index is provided, but it seems to me that this would only be used after a first reading of the book from cover to cover, if readers wanted to go back and refresh their minds about a point they remembered.

The non-fiction text also supports the fiction in trying to enlist admiration and respect for the spiders. In this case, this is done by reminding readers of the similarities between spiders and ourselves. Both species spin, mend and catch their food.

Sentences

At the sentence level, the book offers a good opportunity to compare the narrative past tense with the report style's continuous present. The two opening sentences are:

• My brother loved spiders, and so did I.
• House spiders are some of the most common types of spider.

The report is written in scientific, though very accessible, prose. The subjects of the sentences are 'spiders' in general, or 'an average house spider' or 'a spider' or 'the spider' used in a general sense. One sentence tells us 'There are more than thirty thousand kinds …'. This use of 'there' is known to linguists as an 'existential there'. In other words, it tells us that something exists, in contrast to the use of a word in a sentence like 'She lives over there'. Its use suggests that some new information is going to be offered.

In keeping with its scientific tone, spiders are not anthropomorphised at all in this text, except perhaps on one occasion when we are told that 'they don't like holes in their webs'. I'm not sure whether it's a scientific fact that spiders have feelings, but I very much doubt it. No metaphors or similes are used in talking about them. Two sentences stand out as different from the rest. They are used to make a direct address to the reader. In the imperative mood, the writer urges the readers:

• Save a spider … place a towel over the side of the bath.

The second example is:

• But if you pick one up, handle it very carefully.

As we might expect, there are many more signs of personal involvement in the narrative syntax. The subject of the sentences is often 'Helen'. Otherwise, they almost all contain a pronoun or a possessive adjective or both:

- My brother and I
- we
- our cousin
- our mum.

Words

The contrast between the scientific prose and the narrative is marked at the word level too. The narrative places huge emphasis on feelings. We are told about these in two ways. There are many occasions when feelings are mentioned directly:

- my brother and I loved
- we were very proud
- she screamed and screamed
- she hated
- my brother liked
- I'm not afraid
- you squealed
- she loved it.

This last example brings the story to a very successful conclusion because it marks Helen's arrival at the point where her cousins were when the story started. Before we reach that point, however, we have also had a good many indirect expressions of feeling. Amongst these are:

- she made us [keep the back door shut]
- we had to [go and play in the garden]
- I didn't mean to [damage the spider's web]
- my brother snorted [at something Helen said].

There is a very slightly more sentimental treatment of the spiders in this text, particularly at the point where it's feared they might have all been swept away. 'Poor little spiders', she said. 'Are they all dead?' Thankfully they are not. We are told 'At least seven or eight spiders were already tiptoeing out. They scuttled up into the corners ...'
The vocabulary of the scientific text is much more restrained.

- An average house spider won't live much longer than ...
- Spiders are protected by ...
- Spiders belong to ...

There are plenty of technical terms for parts of a spider's anatomy, and for different members of the arachnid family: 'palps', 'fangs', 'spinnerets', 'tailed whip scorpion' are some examples. As I have said before in an earlier chapter, there is no reason why young children would be put off by these terms. They may not remember them, or be able to spell them, but they will find them fascinating.

An interesting opportunity to compare the fictional treatment of the subject with the scientific comes when the brother indulges in some teasing of his cousin.

- He tried to frighten her by telling her how they suck the juices from flies and other things they catch.

The scientific prose explains this rather gruesome process in a very matter of fact way:

- Spiders can only eat liquid food. They stun their prey with their fangs, then inject a special juice into the body. This turns the insides soft enough for the spider to suck out.

(It is at this point that readers are reminded that we also catch our food.)

Layout

The layout of the book, with fiction on one side of each double page spread and non-fiction on the other, reminds us that there are book conventions which readers must learn and accept. The book is not difficult or confusing to read, especially as each side is written using a different font. Readers are reminded in the index to look for words they are interested in, in both typefaces.

The First Lunar Landing, Rodney Martin, Era Publications 1990

What kind of text is this?

There is no blurb on the covers of this book. The front and back covers form part of the contents. The front shows a photograph of Neil Armstrong making the lunar landing and the back cover provides a summary of the Apollo 11 mission in the form of a chart, with a key. The book is chronologically ordered, and it seems unlikely that, on a first reading at least, it won't be read in its entirety, from front to back. However, the contents page provides a clear indication of what each section contains and this and a helpful index provide adequate support for readers who want to refer to information about a specific part of the mission only.

This is a large format book, and pictures and text must therefore be clear and visible at a distance of 11 feet or so. Most of the illustration is in the form of very dramatic large photographs. The text must necessarily be selective. Can we distinguish any principles or purposes which seem to have influenced the selection?

Structuring the text

The writer's first purpose seems to be to establish that this was an American enterprise. The Introduction quotes an American president, John Kennedy, telling the American people that 'this nation should commit itself to … landing a man on the moon'. The dots presumably indicate that something has been cut from the speech. Can we be sure therefore that it now reads as Kennedy (or his speech writers) intended? The words that we do have suggest that JFK regarded it almost as a duty incumbent on the American people to send someone to the moon. Why this should be so is never made clear. One of the least developed sections of text is one labelled 'Lesson from Apollo 11'. It seems appropriate that the noun is in the singular. Rodney Martin seems to have little to offer, other than two facts: the age of the moon, and the fact that tiny coloured beads of glass were one of the things found in the soil samples. Is this significant? Young readers would probably need more help in understanding why.

Perhaps the author's purpose was rather to inspire young readers to a vision of a future in space? Yet the future is only mentioned in one rather bald statement.

• The Apollo mission also showed us that in the future we could travel even farther than the moon.

Facts or feelings?

The main purpose of the text seems to be to give facts and figures about the mission, with the needs of young readers very much in mind. In addition there are some 'human interest stories' chiefly about the astronauts. We are told that they were responsible for naming the sections of their own spacecraft. The connotations of the names, that of the Apollo missions themselves, and the Eagle and Columbia modules are never commented on. We are told the names and ages of the astronauts, and the fact that they were married and had children. We know what they wore and a bit about what they had to eat. In order to relax, they looked out of the window and played music. The writer is at pains to show us that they had a sense of humour. For example, they once tricked the ground controllers by playing a tape of train whistles and noises. The writer seems determined to stress the astronauts' ordinariness. This seems in marked contrast to what similar texts would have emphasised say a hundred years or so ago when readers wanted to believe in the heroic qualities of the explorers they were reading about.

Meeting the readers' needs

Considering that the author only had had a very limited number of words to use, much of the text is very bland and doesn't tell us very much. We are told, for example, that the astronauts 'expected the journey to the moon and back to take eight days'. This statement seems to offer readers promise of something interesting of the 'whereas in fact ...' kind, but in fact we know from elsewhere in the book that the journey took exactly eight days. It had been meticulously planned by the mission controllers to do just that, and nothing went wrong. We are told that the astronauts found some of their training interesting. Again, readerly expectations are aroused – and disappointed! It transpires that the astronauts 'travelled to different places' and 'met the people who made their spacecraft'. We would have liked to meet them too!

There are a number of statements which describe people's feelings. We have seen in *Spider Watching* how feelings can be incorporated successfully with facts in a non-fiction text. The effect in this text is rather different, however. We are told that:

• Sometimes they did not enjoy the training. One reason was that they were often away from their families.

When Armstrong and Aldrin return to the Columbia module, we are told that:

• Collins was excited to see them again.

As the three head back towards Earth, we are told that:

• Everyone [at Mission Control] was very anxious.

These descriptions are irritating because they seem so obvious. Reading should be an active, meaning-making process: good writers leave ample space for readers to engage with the text and draw conclusions from it. In these examples, nothing seems to have been left for readers to construe for themselves.

Perhaps writers of non-fiction for young people feel some anxiety about overloading their readers with information. In fact, one finds oneself wanting more throughout this text. For example, an astronaut is shown in a labelled diagram wearing a gold visor. This seems very exotic and one would like to know why gold was used. We are told astronauts have to learn to 'eat, drink, sleep and even go to the toilet in space'. The word 'even' seems extraordinary, and the whole phrase misleading. The text is coy on the details, though this is an aspect of the enterprise that would interest children.

There *is* plenty of interesting information.

• The lack of gravity comes across vividly, for example, when we are told that Collins turned a spoonful of water upside down, and the water stayed put, and Aldrin floated a ham sandwich across to another astronaut.
• In an interesting 'text within a text' we are given the dialogue which took place between the astronauts and ground control as the Eagle edged down on to the moon's surface. Again there is a nice mixture of the scientific and technical jargon and the human interest: 'You've got a bunch of guys about to turn blue. We're breathing again'.

I'm intrigued as to why Armstrong's famous 'One small step for man …' words are left out.

Writer's hidden purposes

One other of the writer's purposes is discernible, at the end of the book. Until this point, there has been no direct speech from the astronauts, but the last words in the text are a quote from Armstrong:

• the Earth itself is … an odd kind of spacecraft … You've got to be pretty cautious about how you treat your spacecraft.

Again, one wonders about what has been left out. The text reads as an indirect plea to readers to be more environmentally aware.

Punctuation

One interesting aspect is the use of words in quotation marks. These fulfil several purposes.

• Around the word 'Buzz', for example, they indicate the use of a nickname.
• We are told that they could 'crash' their rocket on the simulator – the punctuation indicating that this was only a pretence.
• Another use is illustrated when we are told that Collins invented a technical term, 'barbecue mode', for the process of turning the spacecraft slowly as it travelled, so the sun would not overheat one side of it.

Elision, or the lack of it, is another interesting aspect of punctuation. 'Did not' and 'were not' and 'would not' are printed in full, but the elided form is used in 'couldn't'. Was this one that was overlooked in the editing process, one wonders.

Word choices

Similes are used to give readers a sense of the scale of the enterprise:

• as tall as a 33 storey building
• as powerful as 160 jumbo jet engines
• like trying to hit a pin head across a classroom with a dart
• as tall as a two-storey house.

There are plenty of interesting technical terms, particularly where the large pages are used to good effect to provide clearly labelled diagrams.

What's The Big Idea? Food, **Emily Moore, illustrated by Sophie Grillet, Hodder Children's Books 1999**

What kind of text is this?

Readers are informed by the blurb on the back of this book that it forms part of a series whose overall title is *What's The Big Idea?* and which is described as

- A ground-breaking series for young people which focuses on the hottest issues and ideas around.

The series title and this description are an indication to the reader that this is not a 'report' type of text giving information about food production, statistics, eating habits etc., although all those can be found in it. It is an argumentative text, presenting a point of view. Very few texts are absolutely neutral. All present the writer's point of view to some degree. A writer is someone who has chosen a word or sentence with great care for the impact it might have on a reader. This text, however, has a pronounced bias. Wray and Lewis (1997 p.107) describe this term as 'one we use to refer to the presentation of ideas we do not agree with'. I don't use it in that way here, as I have a lot of sympathy for the views presented. What I mean is that an adult reading the text, with more experience to bring to reading the book than some of the young readers it is aimed at, can see that a very one-sided view of the issues is being presented.

Developing critical reading skills

Because the text is biased by no means implies that it is unsuitable for use in schools, but that it is very important for children to be encouraged to read it critically. It is part of a teacher's job to develop children as critical readers. Being a critical reader means asking searching questions at the text level, such as:

- Why these particular facts?
- Might there have been others which were omitted?
- We might of course get as far as asking "Can I believe these 'facts'"?
- Why has this picture been used?
- Why has the page been laid out in this way?

At the sentence and word levels, readers need continually to ask themselves:

- Why this particular language?
- Could other words have been used instead?
- What would the effect have been then?
- Why this juxtaposition of ideas in this sentence?

It helps readers in approaching an argumentative text if they know something about where the writer is coming from, his or her background or credentials. In the case of this text, no such information is available.

Guiding readers through a text

Readers welcome information which helps them to find what they are looking for in a non-fiction text. This book provides a contents page, but of the eight chapter titles, only half are sufficiently informative to enable me to decide what kind of information they are likely to offer. These are:

• The history of food
• Hunger
• Modern farming
• How safe is the food we eat?

Of the rest, the first chapter is entitled 'Food for thought', and the last three 'Our future', 'Good news!' and 'What next?'. However, skimming and scanning would be perfectly appropriate reading strategies in tackling the text: each chapter can be read as a separate entity.

The writer's view of her readers

An interesting question to ask about non-fiction at the text level concerns the view the writer appears to have of the potential readers.

• How much does she expect them to know already about the subject?
• What terms and references does the writer feel the need to explain?
• How much stamina does she expect her readers to show, as regards such things as amount of detail and use of jargon?

These are useful aspects to consider when choosing non-fiction for the primary classroom.

This text does not patronise its readers. It covers large areas of quite complex argument, but at a brisk pace, without getting bogged down in too much detail. The reader is addressed directly throughout, starting with the opening words of Chapter 1:

• If you're hungry, you probably just take a look in the fridge to see if you can find something tasty to eat!

The writer, on the other hand, never uses the first person singular with reference to herself, so that attitudes and information both tend to come across as authoritative statements rather than as her point of view.

Fact or opinion?

Another important skill in reading non-fiction is to be able to distinguish clearly between fact and opinion. In order to do this in this text, it's important to look carefully at the sentence structure. Under a heading 'The way forward?' the author writes:

> In the UK, out of 19 million hectares of agricultural land, 15.3 million (80%) are used directly or indirectly (i.e. for animal food) for meat and dairy. A much better idea would be to cut the number of animals kept by a quarter, to keep herds of cows and sheep on grass and for all pigs and chickens to become free range. The manure of this many animals would not be a problem, instead a bonus as it would be used to maintain the fertility of the soil which could be put to good use growing vegetables, fruits, pulses and grains.
>
> Britain could feed itself on a third of its agricultural land if we were all vegetarian.
>
> With the rapidly rising population, it looks as if the future will be much more vegetarian – or there might not be a future at all.

Presumably, the first sentence is a fact. In the second, there is a clue that we have shifted to opinion, 'a much better idea', but the opinion is asserted almost as a fact. Possibly, it is a fact that a vegetarian Britain could feed itself using a lot less land, but a lot of other issues seem to have been left unexplored in making this statement. There are some signs of tentativeness in the grammar of the last sentence – 'it looks as if' and 'there might not be' – which indicate if one is reading closely that these are the writer's opinions.

Textual bias

To leave areas of fact unexplored is as much a sign of bias in a text as to use persuasive or emotional language in supporting an idea. There are two other places where this occurs. One is in a discussion of colonialism, which is defined as 'when one richer country takes over another poorer country'. I am not altogether proud of my country's colonial past, but I think today's children should know about the history of the British Empire. Instead we are told that 'Europeans' came to colonise 'developing countries'. The specific example given is of the Spanish, who 'used their guns to colonise most of central America. This is typical of colonisation … By the 19th century European countries had colonised almost every country in the world …' Now in spite of Maastricht, membership of the EEU etc., etc., I wonder whether British children will see their own country as being involved in all of this. It seems to me dishonest in a book published in Britain to make no specific mention of Britain's colonial past. Similarly, under a heading 'The sickening slave trade' we are told 'When the Portuguese settled in Brazil in the mid 16th century, they set up vast sugar plantations but didn't have enough people to work on them. The slave trade began. The Portuguese shipped out slaves from Africa to Brazil to work on the plantations. Other colonisers followed their idea ...' Again, no hint at all that prominent among these were British colonisers.

As I have said, the fact that there is bias in a text does not, in my view, make it one to avoid. Instead it should be seen as throwing into clear relief questions about reading which need to be frequently raised. These might include 'What are the author's credentials' and 'What is her purpose in writing this text?'

Syntax and word choices

At the word and sentence level, the text is varied and lively. There are several examples of short 'texts within the text' which provide the author with opportunities to structure the sentences in an interesting variety of ways. In a section on animal cruelty, for example, information is put into the mouths of 'Petronella the Pig', 'Charlotte the Chicken' and 'Calvin the Calf'. First person writing can be used therefore to put across a lot of information, some of it quite technical, in an amusing and reader-friendly way. Readers are told about such things as tether stalls, farrowing crates, fattening houses, battery cages, debeaking and veal crates.

Reading charts and diagrams is another important part of accessing non-fiction: in a section on land ownership dealing with issues such as who has enough to eat and who may have a surplus to sell, we meet Vikram, Vatsala and Ali. In order to understand the situations they find themselves in, readers must interpret a diagram, for which a key is provided.

Slang

At the word level, one is most aware of the prevailing 'chatty' tone, with a lot of colloquial and slang expressions. I have said in a previous chapter that slang is a good marker of generation gaps. I am still just sufficiently short of geriatric to know that 'finding something tasty to eat' doesn't mean quite the same thing it did in my day. However, I really felt my age when I read 'If you're grossed out by genetic engineering ...'. Readers are exhorted to 'Hold it right there!' and told 'You might well worry ...'. However, because she has established such a friendly approach, the author seems able to switch from time to time to passages containing a lot of technical information and vocabulary, without this seeming in any way threatening or tedious. In a section on genetic engineering for example, she writes:

• *Halophytes* are plants that do survive well in salty environments. If scientists could take the right gene from the halophyte and put it into a basic food crop such as wheat, maybe it could survive in salty soils.

Sometimes she is able to mix the colloquial and the technical in the same sentence:

• Foraging societies tend to be pretty equal (they are known as egalitarian societies).

I think this is a style which will appeal to the readership for which it's intended.

Text layout

The pages are crowded with information in a variety of formats and typefaces, and with cartoon-like drawings. One could count on one hand the number of pages full of continuous print, in the same font throughout. In one instance, when the reader does come upon one of those, it has a border of tankers, tractors, trains and coal wagons round it. I feel that these features will appeal to the intended readership.

The style in which this book is written and presented makes it a lively, accessible and yet challenging read for Key Stage 2 children. The content will hopefully give rise to some fierce debate.

Chapter 11

Children's language knowledge: setting targets at text, sentence and word levels

If you are a fairly new recruit to teaching, perhaps not having spent very much time in school so far, you may have been wondering just how much of the language knowledge contained in the previous chapters you will be expected to pass on to children while they are in the primary school. The present government has set a target of 80 per cent of 11-year-olds reaching Level 4 of the National Curriculum for English, by 2002.

Before we look in more detail at what language knowledge at Level 4 represents, remember that level descriptors constitute a selection of language knowledge and skills at a particular point in time made by a group of individuals, only some of whom have regular contact with primary children. You will see when you look at the level descriptors in the National Curriculum, if your common sense does not already tell you, that it is very difficult indeed to rank knowledge about speaking and listening, reading and writing into eight discrete levels, which is what the National Curriculum requires for all subjects.

Expressing anxieties about standards of achievement both in literacy and oracy is a favourite British occupation, fanned from time to time by the media, the heir to the throne, some captains of industry, some university dons and so on and so on. The reality is that it is very difficult indeed to make a realistic assessment of what children should know about language, especially by the age of 11. They still have five years of compulsory schooling ahead of them, some are slow to learn, some are coping with English as a second or third language. While some are still struggling to become independent readers and writers, others have acquired a sophisticated control of the written language system. Most children have the basic patterns of spoken English firmly in place, but possibly lack the confidence to deal happily with a wide range of speech situations, especially ones where there is strong pressure to use formal standard English.

Level 4: is it a reasonable assessment for children at the end of primary schooling?

Levels of achievement in English at Key Stage 2, particularly by boys, have been causing particular concern in recent years. Part of the reason for some of the fairly low assessments is that these Key Stage 2 tests were the last ones to become compulsory. Teachers have had relatively little experience of implementing them. I believe that SATs at both key stages are reasonable tests of reading and writing. They have done much to broaden teachers' views of how achievement at each key stage should be measured and so they have had some influence on the kinds of language experiences offered to children. I think this development still has some way to go in Key Stage 2.

The national test for English for 11-year-olds has four components – reading, writing, spelling and handwriting – though the marks are aggregated so that each child receives just one mark for 'English'. If we look at the national figures for reading and writing separately, it emerges that the marks for writing are lower than those for reading. In 1997, for example, 63 per cent of 11-year-olds reached Level 4 or above; of these, 67 per cent reached Level 4 in the reading test, but only 53 per cent in writing. In 1998, the reading figure had improved, with 71 per cent achieving Level 4, but the writing figure stayed the same at 53 per cent. If the 1997 figures are broken down by gender, we find that, of the 53 per cent who obtained a Level 4 for writing, 62 per cent were girls, and only 44 per cent were boys. In reading, there was a 9 per cent gap between girls and boys. It is not unusual for girls, overall, to be ahead of boys in academic achievement at the age of 11, but in the past, boys have tended to catch up during secondary schooling. Nowadays, the girls tend to stay ahead. For the sources of these statistics, and suggestions for further reading on gender differences and literacy, please see the chapter notes.[1]

There has been some variation in the national tests in almost every year since they began, and this will almost certainly continue, but an overview of the requirements in the last few years might be useful with particular emphasis on what has been expected of children in order to achieve Level 4.

SATS at Key Stage 2: an overview

Reading non-fiction

In the reading test, children must usually tackle whole texts, or if not, substantial extracts. Sometimes information is conveyed in photographs, illustrations, diagrams and so on. In each case, it is important that children recognise the type of text they are being asked to read. Issues they might be asked to consider include the following.

At the text level

- Is the text suitable for its purpose and audience?
- What evidence can the child select to demonstrate this? (This must frequently be drawn from several parts of the text.)
- Can the child infer/deduce meanings, opinions, values, attitudes, not explicitly stated in the text?
- What typographical decisions has the writer or publisher made? (Examples might include words printed in bold or in italics.)
- How does the text shape and layout support the reader? (Is the text in large blocks? In segments? In paragraphs? Why?)

At the sentence level

- Is the text written in whole sentences or bullet points? What is the reason for the choice?
- Why has the writer chosen a particular tense, voice or mood?
- What is contributed by the illustrations and diagrams?
- Can the reader interpret information presented in diagrammatic form?

At the word level

- Why has the writer chosen a particular word?
- What alternatives were there?
- What difference would it have made to the meaning to choose one of these?

Reading fiction

When reading a fictional piece children must show an awareness of the type of text they are reading. They must be aware of the differences, for example, between the structure and style of myths, legends, traditional tales and fairy stories. By and large the national tests have avoided the worst aspects of traditional comprehension exercises. Many of my readers will probably remember those weekly episodes, when, faced with a brief extract, without any context at all, usually taken from a book of such extracts, one didn't waste time reading the passage in its entirety, but went straight to the questions, secure in the knowledge that the answer to Question 1 would be found in the first line or two, and would be recognisable because some at least of the words required for the answer matched those of the question. Comprehension exercises of any kind are by no means the most sophisticated way of measuring reader response, but at least these Key Stage 2 tests are conveying the message that that kind of crude matching activity is not what 'comprehending' should mean. Children must show that they have carefully considered what it is they are being asked, and then searched for evidence throughout the text. As well as looking for matters of fact of the 'who', 'when', 'what', 'why', 'where' kind, readers might be required to identify the narrator, saying whether the piece is told in the first or third person.

Learning to read between the lines

Some aspects of the reading test require low-level inference; that is, drawing conclusions from small amounts of information, of a fairly obvious kind. This might perhaps be a straightforward exploration of a character's motives for one particular action. More demanding questions requiring higher level inferential skills would expect readers to scan the text for more information and piece this together in the mind before coming to a conclusion. This might involve commenting on a character, for example, bearing in mind what he or she does and says throughout the story, but also what others, including perhaps the author, say, and how others react towards that character. Sometimes children must deal with conflicting evidence about a character, and show their understanding of why this is the case, in the context of the story as a whole. Higher level inference also might involve teasing out a whole series of causes which have led to a particular effect.

Expressing opinions, forming judgements

Evaluative levels of response to a text involve such things as making personal judgements on characters, explaining, with close reference to the text, why one might want a particular character as a friend, for example. It would be important to show that one had considered advantages and disadvantages. Readers might be asked to comment on what they think might have happened if a particular character had made a different decision. This requires sensitive consideration of what the writer has said about the character. Readers may be asked to judge whether the piece was successful in what it set out to do. Did it hold their attention, and if so, how?

Sentence level issues

At the sentence level, readers must show sensitivity to the writer's choice of sentence length and shape to support meaning. In recent tests, children have been asked to comment on why a series of sentences started with 'and'. Children might be asked to unpick some elliptical utterances – to decipher, that is, some sentences where characters were obviously saying less than they really meant.

Vocabulary choices

At the word level, even perhaps more than when reading non-fiction, it is important for readers to be sensitive to the nuances of words, and to the impact of similes and metaphors. Readers must demonstrate an awareness of how a good writer will show, rather than tell, what a character is feeling, for example, or why a word is especially suitable for the character it is being used to describe. They must be able to say how the setting has been evoked, and what it has to contribute to the impact of the story.

To sum up: what emerges is that by the age of 11, children must be able to demonstrate skills of very close reading, showing an ability to support all statements with close reference to the text, and with appreciation not only of content but of structure and style, bearing in mind purpose and intended readership. All tests have limitations, but I would defend these tests on the grounds that I think they have maintained the correct balance between requiring children to know some of the technicalities of text structure, but most importantly in the context of becoming more sensitive readers. Much depends on the teachers, of course, as to whether this intention is actually realised in each classroom. If teachers spend too much time on practising old test papers rather than giving children wide and varied experience of reading, and drill children in some of the language points I have raised here by means of decontextualised language exercises, then that intention will have been distorted.

The writing test at Key Stage 2

As far as the national writing test is concerned, much depends on children having the ability to recognise the requirements of the particular text type they have chosen. They can choose whether to write a story or a piece of non-fiction. The writing is judged under two headings. The first is purpose and organisation, and the second is grammar, which has two subheadings: punctuation and style. It is very important that the writer demonstrates coherence of approach across all these aspects.

Writing non-fiction

Whilst a great deal of work has been done on story structure, in many Key Stage 2 classrooms, work on non-fiction has been less well developed. Wray and Lewis (1997) found this to be the case in their research[2] and their suggestions about the use of writing frames, described earlier on p.42, should prove to be extremely helpful. The insistence in the NLS framework on the shared and guided reading and writing of non-fiction will also be of great help to children.

Composing text

Children's first obstacle is to recognise the type of text they are being asked to write, and identify its intended audience. They must make decisions about some of the following.

• How will they decide on the overall structure and layout for the piece?
• Will they be able to sustain it throughout?
• Would it be helpful to use subheadings, or ideas grouped into paragraphs?
• What stance will they adopt towards their readers? Will they address them directly or not?

- What decisions can be made about the readers' needs? How much knowledge can be taken for granted? Would readers be able to carry out a procedure from the information offered?
- What kinds of information are most likely to persuade readers to a point of view?
- When is it important to particularise and when to generalise?

Fictional writing

Choosing a story shape
As in any kind of text, coherence is a vital necessity, though the story need not always start at the beginning. Many effective stories work from hindsight. There are other issues writers must face, such as the pace of the narrative, with an effective beginning, a well-developed middle section and a logical end. Characters must be introduced in an interesting way, so as to carry the plot forward. Readers should be able to draw on a variety of evidence in understanding and judging these characters. Readers will expect to be told or to be able to infer, what characters are thinking and feeling, as well as what they are doing.

Sentence structure
As far as grammar is concerned, not surprisingly, to achieve a Level 4 the majority of the sentences used must be correctly demarcated with capital letters and full stops or question or exclamation marks. Commas should be used to separate elements of a sentence, such as phrases, clauses or elements in a list. The apostrophe will be correctly employed. Direct speech should be used effectively, particularly as part of the business of establishing characters and their relationships with each other. Inverted commas will clarify where direct speech begins and ends. Dialogue and action must be neatly interwoven. Children must demonstrate an ability to use complex sentences to present readers with plenty of information; if necessary, that information must be precise, accurate and objective. The use of adverbial phrases and clauses will be expected. Clauses or phrases of time might be used to pinpoint, for example, whether something is a regular event or an unusual occurrence. Children should show the ability to use an appropriate range of sentence connectives, demonstrating order of events, logical connections, emphasis. Pronouns and tenses must be consistent throughout the piece. Use of modal verbs can be difficult to sustain, if children are, for example, writing about what 'will happen', or 'would happen if', or what 'should' or 'might' happen. The passive voice might be chosen, where appropriate.

Getting the words right
Writers need to demonstrate a degree of adventurousness with vocabulary, with well-chosen words making a significant contribution to meaning. They may be able to use some effective metaphors or similes. Some words and phrases should

be chosen for their interest or precision, particularly if some technical vocabulary is required by the topic. Sometimes words will be deliberately chosen for their emotional impact. A child working at Level 4 would show clearly an awareness of the difference between the vocabulary (and for that matter, the grammar) of everyday speech and writing.

How can teachers help?

Children will not be able to achieve the desired level in this test if they have not had wide and varied experience of writing over a number of years. Not only this, but they must have had opportunities to make links between their reading, writing and speaking/listening experiences, opportunities to reflect on how something has been written and how particular structures and devices could be incorporated into their own work. They must have had teachers who have been willing to model writing processes, making explicit the decisions they were making. If necessary, they must have had access to writing frames. They must have had opportunities to edit their work and each other's work. The national tests should not and must not be made ends in themselves. I have described their demands at some length here only because they provide some kind of national bench mark of what is required if government targets are to be achieved.

The National Literacy Strategy

In planning their language work, until now teachers' reference points have been the programmes of study in the national curriculum. But in the shortened forms in which we now have these, they lack specific detail. It has been possible to avoid certain sections altogether, or to convince oneself that they were being done, even if, according to the letter of the document, they were not.

Now for the first time teachers in England have a comprehensive list of learning objectives and set out as they are in the framework document, they make daunting reading, especially at the end of Key Stage 2. Here are just some of the text level requirements.

- Children should be taught to develop skills of biographical and autobiographical writing in role, adopting distinctive voices, for example of historical characters.
- They must be able to write in a journalistic style where appropriate.
- They should be able to construct effective arguments, developing a point logically and effectively, supporting and illustrating points, anticipating possible objections and harnessing the known views, interests and feelings of the audience.
- They should have secure control of impersonal writing, particularly the sustained use of the present tense and the passive voice.

The range of fiction writing expected is also comprehensive.

- Children should be able to manipulate narrative perspective, by writing in the voice and style of a text, or writing a story with two different narrators.
- They should write poems experimenting with active verbs and personification.
- They should study a genre in depth and produce an extended piece of similar writing.
- They should be able to parody a literary text, describing stock characters, plot structure, language and so on.
- They should annotate passages in detail, use a reading journal effectively, write a synopsis.

Getting the syntax right

In order to accomplish this range of texts, the National Literacy Strategy mentions, for example, choosing appropriate connecting words and phrases; exploring how meaning is affected by the sequence and structure of clauses; securing knowledge and understanding of more sophisticated punctuation marks. It suggests that children will need to be able to handle conditional structures – 'if … then …' and 'might', 'could', 'would' and so on – and their uses in deduction, speculation and supposition. The use of the passive voice is likely to be required.

Word choice

At the word level, the framework document is not very successful at linking the learning objectives to the children's own reading and writing, though it does require pupils to practise and extend vocabulary and to experiment with language, for example creating new words, similes and metaphors.

This is only a brief sample, but taken as a whole, the sheer number of learning objectives is worrying. Set out like this, in column after column, there is a danger that they will seem to all but the most confident and determined teachers to constitute a curriculum which is almost entirely 'language product'. By this I mean that it may well appear to teachers that, in order to cover so much ground, separate items of language knowledge must become the learning objectives for their English lessons. Any remnants of 'process', of allowing children to find a voice for what it is they want to say, may be made to serve 'product' ends. I have already been in lessons recently where, for example, children were writing passages describing story settings, knowing full well that they were never going to proceed to the rest of the story. Woe betide the child who was desperate to bring a character in at this early stage. This was a lesson devoted to describing buildings and furniture, pictures, candlesticks. Stairs might creak, but no one was to be described climbing them.

Getting the balance right

It could be argued that there has been too little explicit teaching of writing skills and techniques in recent years. In *The Excitement of Writing*, a very influential book published more than 30 years ago, Mr Alec, later Sir Alec, Clegg was adamant that there is no place for explicit teaching in developing children's writing abilities. He was the director of education for the then West Riding of Yorkshire, and the book consists of examples of children's writing from that LEA with commentaries from their teachers. Children learn to write by writing, Clegg insisted, and by reading 'books of high quality'. But what Alec Clegg was railing against, and quite rightly, was practising aspects of English from what he called 'English exercises'. He and others have sometimes been interpreted as advocating that there should be no 'interference' as I have heard it described, in children's writing, *of any kind*. I think these beliefs have contributed something to some children's low levels of achievement in writing. Explicit teaching of the right kind *can* improve standards.[3] One of the most valuable experiences I have had in my career was working alongside a teacher who was very good at helping children, boys as well as girls, to become accomplished writers. The school was in a mining village in West Yorkshire. Each year she would insist that 'nothing could be done with this class' and each year, their skills and enthusiasm would develop in leaps and bounds between September and July. This was achieved by a lot of good-quality reading, opportunities for talk of all kinds (including drama, teacher modelling, some peer group support), but above all by a lot of one-to-one interaction with the teacher. It is also true to say that, in the old West Riding tradition, creativity of all kinds was valued in that school, especially work in paint and clay and textiles. It was one of the first schools I came across to institute a weekly 'sharing assembly' at which the showing, reading and discussing of children's work was taken very seriously indeed. This was a different climate from the one that now prevails. Above all, it was one in which there was no doubt, with regard to process and product aspects of language work, about which was the servant and which was the master.

Three accomplished writers

In the final section of this chapter I want to look at three pieces of work by three different Year 6 writers. Two of them are boys, and the gender of the third is unknown. I have chosen these pieces because the writers seem to me to be particularly good at using an interesting range of syntax and/or vocabulary to support the meanings they are making. In two cases, this is a personal opinion, and you may feel that you have seen better. It would be very encouraging if you did. In the case of the first piece I have some support for my judgement. It was included in the 1997 DfEE exemplar material, to illustrate for teachers what was required to reach Levels 3–5 at Key Stage 2, and was awarded marks above a Level 4 standard.

An argumentative piece

The writer had been asked to compose a leaflet to be distributed around a local community. Its purpose was to inform people about a piece of land, called The Grove, which was in danger of being spoilt because people were careless when they visited it. The school was organising a petition to 'Save The Grove' by turning it into a nature reserve. The piece was therefore intended to be both informative and persuasive. Some pictures were included which were intended to go in the leaflet.This is what the child wrote. (The spelling and punctuation are as in the original.)

> The Grove is a lovely area of open land, thriving with wildlife but it is in great danger of being spoilt forever if we don't do something about it. A petition has been launched for everyone to sign, to turn the area into a nature reserve. At the moment people are very careless when they visit The Grove. They drop litter everywhere. This spoils the scenary and endangers wildlife. Little animals can get trapped or cut themselves on the things left around.
>
> People on bikes, and walkers, trample down the plants and some people manage to block off the entrance to animals' homes so they get trapped and die. Some people take tape players or just shout and make a lot of noise which scares off animals and spoils other peoples walk.
>
> The Grove is a popular place for dog-owners to take there dogs for walks. Most people don't realise that they're doing any harm when they let their dog of it's lead but dogs often chase small animals and birds and scare them off.
>
> If The Grove was turned into a nature reserve, the animals would be a lot safer. Nesting boxes would be put up which provides safe nesting places for birds. Guided walks would be made so that people could enjoy the wildlife and paths would be made so people don't trample over plants. Information boards would be put up along the walks so people can learn about the wildlife around them.
>
> Some places would be fenced to provide safety from foxes etc. for the animals.
>
> The countryside is something we should all try to protect. It is a valuable part of our lives. It provides a break from the noise and polution of towns and cities and a beautiful place for people to go. It provides homes and food for animals, which are much loved by everyone and it would be a great loss if we were to lose them.
>
> That's why we think you should sign our petition, so that everyone can enjoy the wildlife for generations to come and so that the animals there can live in a safe environment and thrive for years to come. We hope that you will now sign the petition and persuade other people to do so as well so that we can have a beautiful nature reserve for everyone to enjoy.
>
> Thank you.

What is the text trying to achieve?

The purpose of the text is to put forward an argument; the readership is local people who know the area and use it themselves. Among them will be some of those who currently seem to be abusing it, if what the writer says is true. This could be a problem, and another problem for the writer, as a glance at some of the other children's pieces shows, is that this is a plea for something that might or might not happen at a later date. It is tempting, and more straightforward, to talk about the nature reserve as if it was already in existence.

How should it be structured?

A piece of argumentative prose ideally requires an opening statement, which summarises the current situation and states the case that is to be argued. We have a classic example of this in this text: 'The Grove is a lovely area … but it is in great danger … A petition has been launched …'

After this, the writer must marshal some arguments, ideally with sufficient detail to make them convincing to the readers and sustain their interest and attention. This writer does this very cleverly, using a very coherent series of paragraphs. First, the current, rather dismal picture is sketched in. A variety of difficulties are touched on: litter, which spoils the scenery and endangers wildlife; bikes and walkers trampling on plants; dogs chasing animals and birds. Three groups then, are disadvantaged: animals, people and plants.

In the next part of the piece the writer shows how each of these groups could enjoy benefits, if only a nature reserve could be established.

The third section abandons specific detail for something more generally rhetorical, working on peoples' emotions so that when the writer finally summarises the position in a direct address to the reader, 'We think you should sign …', it is likely that they are already reaching for their pens. In case they are still hesitating, the writer cleverly works on their guilt feelings by thanking them for their support.

Cohesion is something the writer can handle in a sophisticated way. After listing the advantages of the countryside, a break from noise and pollution, a place of beauty, homes and food for animals, there is an effective summing up: 'and it would be a great loss if we were to lose them'. The 'them' in this case refers back to everything that has just been mentioned, summing it all up at a stroke. It is an example of what is called anaphoric reference, reminding the reader of clauses mentioned earlier in the text. The writer uses an anaphoric reference again in the last paragraph: 'That's why …' In other words, ' For all the reasons which I have mentioned already earlier in the text'.

Choosing the subjects of the sentences

It's a good idea to make The Grove the subject of the first sentence. It focuses attention on the central issue. The opening sentence has good balance too, with the good and bad prospects neatly linked by 'but'. Sentences are also beautifully balanced in what I have called the rhetorical part of the text. Starting the seventh paragraph with a simple but bold statement, 'The countryside is something we should all try to protect,' the writer builds a series of statements on this, piling them up one after the other – 'It is a valuable part …', 'It provides a break …', 'It provides homes and food …' – until we reach the conclusion from all this: 'It would be a great loss …' The repeated subjects, and a careful use of 'and' make this paragraph build into a powerful plea.

When referring to those who are damaging the environment, the writer obviously doesn't want to point the finger at anyone, and uses the impersonal 'people' as the subject of these sentences. But when he or she arrives at the point where support is being called for, there is a dramatic switch to the first person plural subject and the second person in a direct address to the reader: 'We think that you … We hope that you …' The writer is coy on the subject of who has launched the petition. This is a contrived, not a real situation, and the writer may perhaps feel uncertain of how far to go in inventing details which were not in the original brief. He or she gets round this by using a passive construction: 'a petition has been launched …'

Sentence shape

The writer employs a wide variety of sentence shapes. He or she knows when to keep the sentence simple, for effect, and when to employ a balanced compound sentence. Complex sentences are used to give extra information or to make clear the distinction between what the current situation is, and what it could be. Extra information is offered for example in an adverbial clause: 'People on bikes, and walkers, trample down the plants and some people manage to block off the entrance to animals' homes *so they get trapped and die*'. Pressure is put on readers to sign by giving them lots of cogent reasons, again in adverbial and noun clauses: 'That's why we think that you should sign our petition, so that everyone can enjoy the wildlife for generations to come and so that the animals there can live in a safe environment and thrive for years to come.'

Moods and tenses

Modal verbs are well handled in quite a difficult context. Again the writer chooses passive constructions, rather than stating explicitly who will be responsible for activating the plan, and so there is the double difficulty of 'if…then' constructions in the passive voice. 'If The Grove was turned … animals would be …', 'Nesting boxes would be put up …', 'Guided walks would be made …' The cohesion of the modal verbs is maintained throughout.

Words: speech / writing differences

The writer is aware of the difference between the vocabulary of speech and of writing, and employs more formal synonyms, such as 'thriving' with wildlife, a petition has been 'launched', 'a valuable part of our lives', 'for generations to come'. He or she is also adept at choosing words to play on the emotions: 'spoilt forever', 'people trample down the plants', 'little animals can get trapped'.

In some ways, of course, the piece shows signs of immaturity, but considering the age of the writer, it seems unreasonable not to dwell on the large number of language devices which have been successfully deployed to create an effective piece of writing, especially in a contrived test situation.

Recounting an event

The second piece is a true account of something that happened to the writer, a ten-year-old boy, on a journey from London to Manchester. Although English is his first language, it is not the first language of his parents. Again, the spelling and punctuation have been left as in the original.

Losing My Watch

It was on a bus bound for Manchester that my mum apealled to me for the time. Without further notice I proudly rolled up my sleeve to proudly reveal my digital wristwatch except for the fact that one thing was missing: the watch itself: I must have lost it while frolicking with my friends. I turned away, resisting tears which were welling up behind my eyelashes. I searched my shirt sleeves and cuffs, but all in vain. I felt anger, and for a moment a pang of bitterness shot through my heart. I was asked gently where I had last seen it. The burning dissapointment of losing my watch was still fresh in my mind. I turned away while tears streamed down my cheeks. I looked bleakly at the cars and cycles skillfully weaving thiere way through the bustle of the traffic. I whimpered. The sky was grey around me. Horns hooted. Lorries roared boldly past my window. I remember that moment clearly. The world had no sympathy.

Purpose and audience

This is a type of non-fiction which children usually find much easier to handle than the last one, a personal recount. Readers expect some kind of scene setting, or what is known as orientation, a recount of the events as they occurred, and a closing statement to round things off. One of the things I like about this piece is that the writer *shows* us the situation unfolding, rather than telling us what the problem was. We envisage him on the bus, the appeal for the time, and the awful moment of truth. As the events unfold, we see the scene in detail, and are given a vivid description of the writer's evolving feelings, from pride through to tears, then anger and bitterness and finally, disappointment. He skilfully avoids watering down the emotional impact by keeping the focus on himself: his mother's reaction is very subtly sketched in, in the words 'I was gently asked ...'. Again what makes this unusual as a recount text is that the writer then places his own small tragedy in a wider context. There is something reminiscent of Breughel's famous painting of Icarus, tumbling from the sky because his waxen wings have melted, while all around and beneath him, life goes on as usual, disregarding his plight. Even the weather reflects the mood of the writer: 'The sky was grey around me'. John Ruskin coined the phrase 'pathetic fallacy' for the inclination he felt poets had to suggest human qualities for natural objects, as in 'the cruel sea' and so on. (The term 'pathetic' refers to something arousing feelings, and is nothing to do with the everyday use of the word.) To be honest, the writer here only hints at the sky perhaps reflecting what he himself was feeling, by using the word 'grey' which readers are very ready to link with sadness.

Sentences

At the sentence level, syntactic structures appear to have been chosen to support the writer's intentions. First of all the scene is set, with an unusual subject: 'It was on a bus …' rather than 'We were on a bus'. We are therefore invited to look *at* the bus, with the writer and his mother on it. From then on, however, 'I' is the subject of the majority of the sentences, which concentrates our attention on the writer very firmly indeed. If the subject does vary, it is only to 'The burning diss-apointment' or to those moments at the end when we are shown a cruel, disregarding world: 'The sky was grey …', 'Horns hooted', 'Lorries roared boldly past my window'. These sentences are brutally short, and make for maximum emotional impact, especially the summing up: 'The world had no sympathy'.

There is a bold attempt to use a range of punctuation, such as the colon, which doesn't quite come off as it is used twice in the same sentence.

Choosing the right words

This writer, like the last, can employ literary vocabulary. Examples are 'bound for Manchester', 'appealed to me for the time', 'frolicking with my friends', 'a pang of bitterness shot through my heart'. There is more in a similar vein. When I shared this piece with a group of teachers recently, they could see little merit in it, and said that they would advise the boy to 'tone it down'. I think their comments raise some interesting issues. We are being asked to encourage children to experiment with a range of text types, syntax and vocabulary, and so when they do, it seems unreasonable to criticise them if their efforts seem clumsy and 'over the top'. Many adult writers, painters, sculptors can be seen to have gone through long periods of experimentation before honing down their skills to achieve maximum effect. To know what to take out takes a long time to learn. Just as children have acquired 'primary school habits of writing and speaking' over long years of experience, 'telling our news', 'describing how our chicks hatched', and so on, teachers too I think have internalised patterns of what they hope to find in children's writing. These internalised patterns will not be in all teachers' minds of course, but I suspect they may often be shared across a whole school staff. The teachers with whom I shared this piece favoured simple, sincere, straightforward pieces, apparently written from the heart.

Mulling over these issues, I remembered a piece of story writing by an 11-year-old boy which, when I first read it, had aroused similar critical feelings in me. It was brought to my notice by John Dixon and Irene Farmer when we worked together in the Bretton Hall Language Development Unit, and I am grateful to them for permission to quote it here.

Telling a story

Fred at the Zoo

Fred was very excited. His father had promised to take him to the zoo as a birthday treat. He could take two pals with him. He was going to take Boris because he was his pal and Claude because he could give them the latin names and they could pretend they were very intelligent. Fred zoomed round to Boris's house on his bike. "Hey Boris come on. Dad says I can take you to the zoo, that's the place what people go to, to see what animals are like in their-natural summat or other, come on." "The word is 'habitat'" says snooty Claude coming down the path. "May I come?" "Yer, course, I were just gonna ask you." "I will just get permission from mumsie." He stepped into his Rolls-Royce convertible and zoomed off. Three minutes later he was back. "I have got permission from mumsie." They got there. After twenty minutes of goggling at a python, eight minutes of watching an elephant and twenty-eight pence worth of betting on which mouse will eat the most lettuce leaves in the next twelve point three-four seconds (Claudes watch does everything) they come to the lions. "It is just a big cat" says Claude. In no time at all Fred is inside the cage stroking it. It lets out a great roar and bounds out of the cage. Then follows a great chase in which Clause loses one Rolls Royce convertible through a panicky chauffeur, one private helicopter through the G.P.O's new telephone lines and fifty-eight point five pence through a taxi driver. Fred and Boris, quite oblivious to the danger are having a touch-your-toes contest in a dead-end alley. The lion, trapped by keepers bounces onto Fred's back, leaps over the wall, and is promptly sat on by the elephant. Fred is still saying that he did not collapse but was knocked out by a charging porter.

What is the writer trying to achieve?

This is certainly not written from the heart. It is written to amuse, in a style reminiscent of a traditional comic or a TV cartoon. Both plot and characters are 'over the top' and a large amount of detail is included, in this case not to inform the reader so much as to contribute to the humour. This is especially true where there is a deliberate linking of dire disaster with trivial mishap: 'Claude loses one Rolls Royce convertible … one private helicopter … and fifty-eight point five pence'. The writer can use speech style to convey character, from snooty Claude asking "May I come?" to down to earth Fred, "Yer, course I were just gonna ask you". The text rattles along at a quick pace, with direct speech and narrative well interwoven.

Sentence variety

This boy is able to make good use of sentences of varying lengths, and has the good sense to leave out the 'ands' and 'thens' which would stem the rapid flow of the text. In the longer sentences, he packs in a lot of information without holding up the flow. He does this by skilful use of phrases, clauses and punctuation. This is especially true in the sentence 'After twenty minutes of goggling at a python, eight minutes of watching an elephant and twenty-eight pence worth of betting on which mouse would eat the most lettuce leaves in the next twelve point three-four seconds …'. The adverbial phrases are being deliberately overloaded with specific detail to make them funny. The bracket '(Claudes watch does everything)' is cleverly used to add an 'aside' to this great overload of information. There is a switch of tense halfway through the piece, from past to present. It's hard to be sure whether this is deliberate. I suspect it is, because each half is consistent, and the switch is made at just the moment when the narrative benefits from a 'moment by moment' comment, after the scene setting of the first half.

Of course, there are very many children who, when the time comes to leave primary school, are still not secure in handling some of the more complex devices of written English. There are plenty whose writing is still close to speech, and some who still can't handle the writing system or the punctuation system beyond the most rudimentary levels.

These three writers each show considerable abilities in managing the resources of the English language at text, sentence and/or word levels, to support the meanings they are exploring. I don't think that they are necessarily writing from the heart but I think they are enjoying what they are doing. They are 'trying out their language wings' as it were, and now and again, to pursue that metaphor, they will fall flat on their faces. But I don't think, with great respect to the teachers who advised 'toning it down' that this is the way forward. If we insist on writers being too introspective, or if we have too rigid a view of any kind of the styles of writing we want from a class, we may discourage children from experimenting with language in just the same way as we can by too much emphasis on spelling and punctuation in the early stages of composition. It's worth the odd purple patch along the way surely, to encourage those children who have the confidence to experiment, to widen their language repertoires.

Chapter 12

Conclusion

It will have become apparent, if you have read the book thus far, that in describing language knowledge, whether at text, sentence or word level, I have tried very hard to include both speaking and writing. They are not identical at any of these three levels, though there are large areas of overlap. Ron Carter (1994) claims that understanding the differences between speech and writing is one of the most important aspects of language knowledge for teachers, and I agree with this. What cannot be disputed, it seems to me, is that speaking and writing are of equal importance. I have heard it said recently that the literacy hour 'has put speaking and listening on the back burner'. This is nonsense.

It is not easy for schools as social institutions to provide opportunities for pupils to participate in the full range of speech situations they will meet in life. Drama can go some way towards extending the range, but even here, there are limitations. There are two types of speaking and listening, however, which schools are ideally set up to provide opportunities for. One is talking to learn: to identify a question or an issue; to explore it; to share ideas with others; to reflect on what has been learned and to think about how one can apply the learning, all the time building up one's confidence in oneself as a learner. The second is talking to build and maintain the life of the community, in this case, the school. This includes learning to explore aspects of one's own and others' behaviour; to make decisions with others; to negotiate over rules and practices. The literacy hour, with its whole class, interactive teaching and learning, its group work and plenary sessions, offers ideal opportunities to develop the first of these, and to some extent, the second too, when one considers some of the managerial aspects of this approach to teaching and learning.

Speaking and listening is too much a part of everyday life, of the way we negotiate our relationships, our jobs, our hobbies and interests above all our sense of ourselves and our place in the world, for schools to contemplate opting out of giving it equal care and attention.

This brings me to the second point I want to emphasise in this concluding chapter. The roots of the language are in everyday speech. Steven Pinker (1994, p.7) makes the point well when he says:

There is a world of elegance and richness in quotidian speech that far outshines the local curiosities of etymologies, unusual words and fine points of usage.

This respect for the significance of the language we all use to carry out our daily lives is at the heart of what I think is important in developing language knowledge. In 1964, Alec Clegg, in *The Excitement of Writing*, wrote:

A minority of pupils in the schools of this country are born into families whose members speak *the normal language* of educated society ... There are, however, other children, *possibly a majority in industrial areas*, who have to learn *this acceptable language* at school but who, in some cases, may well face discouragement, or even derision, if they venture to use it at home. (p.1, my italics)

I find this way of thinking completely unacceptable. It seems extraordinary, looking back over the 35 years since the book was published, that Alec Clegg, who believed so passionately in bringing out the talents of every child in the old West Riding schools, could have written them. It seems to me that any society that is prepared to write off the language of the majority of its citizens as 'abnormal' or 'unacceptable' is in a very perilous state. This is not for one moment to deny that there is such a thing as slovenly or incorrect speech and writing produced in any dialect, standard or non-standard.

We start out, each one of us, by learning the spoken language of our home and of our community. These, to return to my metaphor, are our language roots. If I could develop the metaphor briefly: we are very fortunate that the 'tree' of the English language, developed and enriched over hundreds of years, has very many branches. Some of them are a great way off the ground, but they are accessible to those who are prepared to scramble up. In Chapter 11 I described some children who, it seemed to me, had wanted to see what is was like to try out some of those 'branches' of language. If they get stuck or fall off in doing so, our job is not to tell them off and bring them back to safety, but to give them better scrambling skills.

To acquire more knowledge about the construction of texts, the structure of sentences, the choice of words, is to be empowered as a speaker, listener, reader or writer. Teachers can only pass on knowledge about these language systems if they are secure in them themselves. That is their first task. What follows is very, very much more difficult: to find the right ways to pass the knowledge on to pupils. This has been a book about the first phase: the development of language knowledge. I would like to end with some thoughts about how the pupils might benefit in the next stage, because that, in the end, is what really matters.

a learner by taking part in rule-governed social behaviour may pick up the rules by means hardly distinguishable from the processes by which they were first socially derived – and by which they continue to be amended. On the other hand, along may come the traditional teacher and, with the best intentions, trying to be helpful, set out to observe the behaviour, analyse to codify the rules and teach the outcome as a recipe. Yes, this may sometimes be helpful, but as a consistent pedagogy it is manifestly counter-productive ... We have a choice: we can operate so as to make [the classroom] as rich an interactive learning community as we can, or we may continue to treat it as a captive audience for whatever instruction we choose to offer. (Britton 1994, p.263)

Appendix 1

Auditing your language knowledge

Auditing what you know about a subject can be a rather depressing, even a frightening undertaking, and so I would like to make one or two points before you begin.

- I presume that you are reading this book because you are hoping to be a primary teacher, or maybe you are already teaching in Key Stage 1 or 2. In my view, the question you continually need to keep in mind therefore, as you audit your language knowledge, is 'Do I know enough to help me to enthuse and excite children to extend and develop their experience of language?' You may be tempted to answer 'No!' to this question, but as you go on, you're very likely to find that you know more than you think you do. Part of your negative response may come from feeling that you don't have the right terminology in which to describe what you know. Terminology is not the most important aspect of language study, though it can serve a useful purpose. (See (d) below, 'Putting into words what we know about language'.)
- Because you are teaching children in the early stages of schooling, this does not mean that a very basic level of language knowledge will suffice. (See Chapter 1 of this book for some discussion of how much you need to know.)
- However, the uses you will make of your language knowledge are different from those say, an academic linguist or a grammarian would be concerned with. There are people whose life work is the study of phonology or syntax and there are others who will spend many a happy hour writing to the newspapers about a perceived abuse of a grammatical rule. Your position, I suggest, is different from either of these. Above all, your task is to foster in children the wonder and excitement to be had from sharing a text, or from making one themselves.

The difficult issues arise when you try to decide specifically what you need to do, to foster this excitement. It's not just a question of what you as a teacher come to know about language, but how skilful you are in interacting with the children you teach. What kinds of 'knowing about language' will increase the children's language powers, which are already impressive even before they come to school? Are there some kinds of language teaching which might even get in the way of the children's development? Before you tackle the activities on specific aspects of language, you could begin by thinking about some important aspects of the primary teaching context you will be working in. You will find my commentary on this activity on p.160.

Activity 1: setting the primary teaching context

Try making a few notes under four broad headings:

(a) Home/school contrasts.
 What would you say are the similarities and contrasts between the kinds of language a child uses at home and the language demands of school? (Think about the purposes for talk/who does the talking/what do they know about each other?)
(b) Speech/writing contrasts.
 Think about some of the speaking – and writing – you have done in the last few days. What similarities and contrasts can you think of between the spoken and written language you used on these occasions?
(c) Language as a process and language as a product.
 What kinds of language skills and knowledge are you as an adult drawing on, probably without even thinking about it, which enabled you to do that speaking and writing? Which aspects of the speaking or writing were the most difficult for you? Why was that?
(d) Putting into words what we know about language.
 How could you turn what you know implicitly about language into explicit knowledge so that you could share it with children? Similarly, what would you need to do to help them to share what they know implicitly, with you and with each other?

Why not take 20 minutes or so to consider these questions? See if you can jot down two or three points in response to each one. Don't worry if you can't manage as many points as that at this stage. You will find ideas to help you as you read the chapters of this book. You could try the activity again after you have read some of them, and I hope that then you will feel that you have developed your thinking.

Levels of language study

If you plan to teach in England, and sometimes this applies to Wales too, you will find yourself referring to the National Literacy Strategy as the basis for your language planning. In the NLS, language knowledge is grouped under three headings, at text level, sentence level and word level. In their daily lives, children are used to encountering language most often in the form of texts,[1] and the text level is a good place from which to start some detailed language work. For most of us, it's at the text level that we get the most fun, enjoyment or use from our reading and speaking. But we need to help children to think about what lies behind the construction of a text.

Most children will not have given much consideration to why writers or speakers choose to structure their texts in a particular way, why they might opt for a particular sentence shape or go for one word rather than another. What is the effect of these choices on the meanings being made? Perhaps this is not something you have ever considered very closely. This sentence and word level work is most successful when firmly rooted in the reading and writing of texts so that children are not looking at each level of work in isolation from the others.

The remaining activities will give you opportunities to assess some of your current language knowledge at each of these levels.

Activity 2: text level study

Please read the following extract carefully. The questions I am asking you to think about are to help you consider your own knowledge about texts and are not necessarily in the form you would use if you were raising these issues with children.

WHAT WERE DINOSAURS?

What would it have been like to have lived when dinosaurs ruled the earth? No book can really show you. You have to use your imagination. Imagine the ground shaking under your feet as a herd of 10,000 Triceratops stampedes towards you. Imagine the sound of a five-tonne duckbill dinosaur calling to his mate with its long, trombone-like head crest. Imagine the sight and smell of a herd of 40-tonne Brachiosaurus in a conifer forest, pine needles showering down from their munching mouths, 14 metres above you. Dinosaurs lived millions of years ago, long before humans existed. Scientists who studied the fossil bones of dinosaurs thought they must have been giant, cold-blooded reptiles. They saw them as slow-moving, stupid 'mistakes' which died out to make room for the superior mammals. Recent discoveries have shattered this view. We now know that dinosaurs were a great success.   (Theodorou 1995)

(a) How would you sum up the author's main purpose in writing this text? At what point in your reading does this become apparent? If you had the book in front of you, do you think there would be other indications of the purpose of the text?

(b) Do you think the author had particular readers in mind? What evidence would you draw on?

(c) In terms of its structure and syntax, the piece falls into two roughly equal parts. At what point in the text would you say the second part begins?

(d) How would you describe, in general terms, what the author is trying to do
   – in the first part of the text?
   – in the second part?

(e) From what you have said so far about the text, what categories of content do you predict will be found in some of the book's eight chapters?

(f) As well as chapter headings, what do you think the book will contain which will help readers to access the material successfully?

See p.160 for a commentary on this activity and a guide to further reading.

Activity 3: identifying text types

It's difficult to decide how many types of text there are (see pp.34 to 42). For example, how many different types of story can you think of? On what basis are you classifying them? There are very many ways of structuring a story. The structures of fictional texts are, however, generally quite distinct from non-fictional ones. Research has shown that there are six non-fiction types of text which occur very frequently in everyday life (see p.41) It therefore would probably be helpful to children to introduce them to examples of each of these and to support them in creating their own.

To help you to think about some of the characteristics of these text types, see if you can match each of the opening lines below to its appropriate label. They are jumbled up at present. Think carefully in each case about the evidence you are drawing on.

(a) Make a nose using papier mâché, paint or sticky paper, a piece of an egg box, a bottle cork or button.	novel
(b) When the cocoa beans are dry, they are packed into sacks and taken to the buying station.	personal recount
(c) Now then, I was twelve, rising thirteen, when our Daniel got killed. Aye…it was a long time ago. I'm talking about a time of day eighty-three years back. Eighty-three years. It's a time of day that's past your imagining.	persuasive piece
(d) In my opinion, school uniform should be abolished.	poem
(e) The wind was a torrent of darkness among the gusty trees, The moon was a ghostly galleon, tossed upon cloudy seas.	explanation

(f) Our class enjoyed our trip to Chester Zoo and   instructions
we would like to go again.

See p.162 for a commentary on this activity and a guide to further reading.

Activity 4: sentence level work

(a) What kind of sentence is each of the following?
1. *What would it have been like to have lived when dinosaurs ruled the earth?*
2. *Our class enjoyed our trip to Chester Zoo and we would like to go again.*
3. *Make a nose using papier mâché.*
4. *Let them enjoy a long and prosperous life!*

(b) Identify each of the sentences in (a) as simple, compound or complex.

(c) Punctuation.
Very few sentences consist of combinations of single words. An example of one that does would be *'I live here'*. It's more usual to find 'chunking' of words with some, though by no means all, of the chunks marked by some form of punctuation. An example would be *'I / have lived / in London / for many years'*.
  I've rewritten one of the dinosaur sentences below, leaving out the punctuation.
1. Indicate by a line where you think the chunks might begin and end.
2. Punctuate the passage.

   Imagine the sight and smell of a herd of 40-tonne Brachiosaurus in a conifer forest pine needles showering down from their munching mouths 14 metres above you.

3. Here is another reconstruction from the same text. What do you think about the changes I have made to the punctuation, replacing the full stop after 'view' with a comma?

   Recent discoveries have shattered this view, we now know that dinosaurs were a great success.

(d) Which voice is being used in the underlined part of the sentence (active or passive?)?

   'When the cocoa beans are dry, <u>they are packed into sacks</u>.'

(e) From the sentences in Activity 3 identify
1. an imperative verb
2. a modal verb
3. a verb in the infinitive.

(f) Word classes (you may be used to calling these 'parts of speech').
When you are deciding which class of words a particular example belongs to, it's very important to look at the word in the context of the other words around it. For example, you met this sentence in Activity 2:

   'No book can really show you.'

1. What class of words does 'book' belong to here?
2. Can you put the word 'book' into two other sentences, in each of which it belongs to a different class of words?

(g) Standard and non-standard Englishes.
Would you say that you spoke using standard English? Sometimes? Always? Do you use standard English when you are writing?

1. Are you clear about what the term refers to?
2. Explain the difference between accent and dialect.
3. In extract (c) in Activity 3, what language features suggest that the novel is written in a regional dialect?

See p.162 for a commentary on this activity and a guide to further reading.

Activity 5: word level work

I've made the point already that in my view developing an enthusiasm for language is your most important task. It is this which will inspire the children you teach. An important part of this is feeling excited about words – not afraid of them, not worried in case you spell them wrongly first time, but keen to explore their meanings, enjoy the sound and the shape of them and experiment with them in your own work. Some of you may have had this enthusiasm since you were children; some may feel that this is the hardest thing of all to achieve. It's very important that you try.

(a) Poetry is one of those types of text which many people love but others hate (or think they do). If you are one of the latter, try just for a few minutes reading the following (very brief!) extract from *The Frozen Man* by Kit Wright, and do your best to find two points about the words he uses which lift the poem above the excitement level of a note to the milkman.

> Out at the edge of town
> where black trees
> crack their fingers
> in the icy wind
> and hedges freeze
> on their shadows
> and the breath of cattle,
> still as boulders
> hangs in rags
> under the rolling moon,
> a man is walking
> alone:

(b) The origins of words is something else that you might develop your interest in. Where do you think these come from?

1. chocolate; 2. tattoo; 3. hubbub; 4. lady.

(c) In teaching children to read you will need to be confident in your ability to segment words, that is, to split them up, in a number of ways. You will learn with experience what kind of segmentation is most helpful to a child on any one occasion. Here are some examples to start you thinking:

1. Segmentation into phonemes:
    Say the word 'bread' aloud. Think carefully about how many sounds you can hear.

2. Segmentation into onset and rime:
    Look at and listen to this group of words: what do you think would be the most useful 'word splitting' activity to suggest to a child in this case?

    bread; head; lead; dead.

3. Segmentation into morphemes:
    Look at this group of words. How might you do the segmenting this time?

    leader; leading; leads; mislead.

4. Segmentation into syllables:
    'Leader' has two syllables (we can clap two beats, as it were). 'Leads' has one. Using the children's names is a good way in to some work on syllables. Think of some one, two and three syllable names you might use to practise syllabification.

(d) In Activity 2 above, we had 'lead' rhyming with 'dead' and 'head.' However, 'ea' can sound quite different, as in the sentence 'Follow my leader.' The English spelling system is very complex. There is not always a one-to-one correspondence between a sound and the way that sound is written down. To understand more about this, try to think of three other ways of making the vowel sound you can hear after the 'l' in 'leader'.

See p.165 for a commentary on this activity and a guide to further reading.

It would be impossible in this one audit to cover all the areas that you will need to know about. My intention rather is to highlight the areas in which you will need to become proficient, with some pointers towards the range of issues within each one.

I hope that working through these activities will have raised some interesting questions for you about levels of language use, and the relationships between them, and that you will enjoy pursuing the answers.

Commentaries

Activity 1

(a) Home/school contrasts: you might like to compare your ideas with what is said in Chapter 3 of this book.

(b) Speech/writing contrasts: see pp.30–31 and 57–8.

(c) See Chapters 4 and 5 for discussion of what we know about texts; Chapters 6 and 7 explore aspects of grammatical knowledge; Chapter 8 looks at word level knowledge.

(d) Chapters 4 to 8, as described above, contain some of the terminology we can use to share and extend implicit knowledge. However, please remember my warning that the teaching of terminology is not the most important aspect of your work. Pupils parroting terms they only half understand would be a retrograde step in their language development. Above all, as a teacher you must try to devise what Helen Bromley (2000) calls 'shared contexts for the joint creation of fresh understandings' (p.2). She has some helpful suggestions to make on how this can be done. You must think very hard about the part some language terminology shared by pupils and teachers might play in building these contexts.

Activity 2

(a) 'Purpose' is a key concept in discussing texts but a tricky one. An author can have many purposes for writing a single text: to inform, to amuse, to excite, to curry favour with someone – to make money even! Here we are only concerned with the function or purpose of the words themselves, and not any underlying considerations.

- The extract suggests that the text was primarily designed to inform its readers – to give them information about dinosaurs. This would put it, in NLS and National Curriculum terms, into the category of 'report' texts. For more information, see pp.40–1.

- The title of the text provides the first clue as to the type of text it will be. There are also clues in the illustrations on the front cover, and in the blurb on the back. Children need to develop their skills in selecting texts which will be appropriate for their purposes and should have their attention drawn to these features from a very early age. In approaching both fiction and non-fiction texts, they should learn to look for the names of authors, publishers and series they have met before and found enjoyable.

(b) There is evidence to suggest that the book was written for young readers. This includes:
  - the grammatical form chosen for the opening sentence
  - the direct address to the reader in several of the sentences
  - the exhortation to imagine what it was like to be alive at the time, using the senses as a way in
  - the use of some informal vocabulary such as 'munching mouths'
  - the amount of detail the writer includes: enough to interest and inform, but not as much as an adult or specialist reader would require. 'Scientists who studied...' is an example. A specialist reader would not be content with this degree of vagueness but would expect chapter and verse on which scientists and when.

(c) There seems to be a change in the structure of the text when the author gets to 'Dinosaurs lived millions of years ago...'

(d) In general terms, the first part of the text seems to be directly addressed to the readers, urging them to imagine what it would have been like to live at the time of the dinosaurs. The second part switches to providing the readers with facts and figures about dinosaurs.

(e) If you have seen this as an informative text, rather than, say, a story about dinosaurs, you will probably be expecting more about such things as:
  - what types of dinosaur there were
  - what they ate
  - how and where they made their homes
  - why they became extinct.

All these points are covered in the book. It is an important part of the teaching of reading from Key Stage 1 onwards to encourage children to go to texts with clear expectations of what they will find in them. Sometimes it's helpful to get children to formulate some questions before they start to read the text.

(f) We access many non-fiction texts differently from the way we read stories and poems, not always starting at the beginning and reading through to the end. In locating the bits of information we want, we find the following helpful:
  - contents pages
  - headings and sub-headings in bold type
  - information in boxes, sometimes with a different coloured background from the rest of the page
  - indexes

- diagrams, pictures, etc., which stand out clearly from the pieces of written text.

Inevitably, some of the vocabulary used will be quite specialised. Glossaries are useful in explaining technical terms.

An introduction to all of the above also forms part of reading instruction from the early years.

Activity 3

(a) is from a text giving *instructions* on how to make a puppet. The verb in the imperative would be a strong clue here: instructional texts are telling us to do something.

(b) is part of an *explanation* of how chocolate is made.

(c) might have been a personal recount: we can hear the voice of the speaker coming through strongly, telling us his story. In fact, it is from a novel, *Isaac Campion*, by Janni Howker, written in the first person.

(d) is from a child's piece of writing, *persuading* us to consider an issue from her point of view.

(e) is the opening two lines of the poem, *The Highwayman* by Alfred Noyes. Rhyme, rhythm and figurative language combine to make this extract easy to recognise.

(f) is another piece written by a child, *recounting* what happened on a school trip.

If you were able to recognise these short extracts, it was because as an adult you have come across texts like these before – you 'know how they go'. For a more detailed look at some of the syntactic and lexical choices which might have prompted your decision, see Activities 4 and 5 below.

Activity 4: sentence level work

(a)
1. is a question. It's a good idea to use this type of sentence as the opening of a factual text for young readers. It may engage their attention and stimulate some imaginative involvement.
2. is a statement.
3. is an instruction.
4. is an exclamation.

(b)
1. a complex sentence;
2. a compound sentence;
3. a simple sentence;
4. a simple sentence.

This is an area of grammar that many people claim to find difficult to discuss explicitly, though all of us use a variety of these sentence structures quite spontaneously from a very young age. See Chapter 7 for more information.

(c) Punctuation

1. One way of dividing the passage into chunks would be as follows:

   Imagine / the sight and smell / of a herd / of 40-tonne Brachiosaurus / in a conifer forest, / pine needles showering down / from their munching mouths, / 14 metres above you.

2. To some extent the position and the number of commas is a matter of the writer's judgement. A colleague who sometimes used to act as a response partner for me tells me that I use far too many! You might have felt that you wanted to add a comma after 'Brachiosaurus' but omit the one after 'munching mouths'.

3. In the second reconstructed sentence,

   Recent discoveries have shattered this view, we now know that dinosaurs were a great success.

the comma is not as satisfactory as the full stop. Some reasons for this are as follows:

   – Each part, before and after the comma, constitutes a clause in its own right, because each has its own subject and a verb.
   – It's true that the ideas in the two clauses are related but each idea has been expressed in a way that makes it syntactically independent. The two parts are of equal weight; neither is 'subordinate' to the other. We have two main clauses here.
   – The two clauses could have been linked by a coordinating conjunction, such as 'and':

   Recent discoveries have shattered this view and we now know that dinosaurs were a great success.

   – Writers have important decisions to make about whether to let their sentences stand alone, or to make them flow into each other. The use of conjunctions, such as 'and' is only one way of joining parts of a text together. This area will be an important part of the work on writing you do with children. See pp.82–4 if you would like to find out more.
   – If the second clause is allowed to stand alone, after a fairly substantial pause provided by a full stop, it provides a more dramatic conclusion to the whole of the second part of the text, enticing the reader to go on and find out more.

You should ensure that you are confident about the use of other types of punctuation such as apostrophes, question marks and speech marks. The teaching of punctuation will be an important part of your work with children. Trainees on ITT courses in England are now required to pass tests to ascertain their level of skills in punctuation, as well as spelling, comprehension and grammar. If you would like to know more about punctuation, you can find help by using the index of this book. A particularly useful publication is *Computerised skills tests in literacy: guidance for trainees*, published by the Teacher Training Agency (no date).

(d) Passive. The cocoa beans are having something done to them by someone (not specified). The purpose of this text, as we have seen, is to explain the chocolate-making process. Cocoa beans are central to this, and presumably the writer wants to keep our attention firmly focused on them, and not on the people engaged in carrying out the process. Using the passive enables the writer to keep 'cocoa beans' as the subject of the sentences. (See pp.58–61 if you would like to find out more about the construction of sentences.)

(e) Make [sentence (a)]; should [sentence (d)]; to go [sentence (d)].

(For more information, see pp.66–72.)

(f)
1. In this sentence, 'book' refers to an object you can see, touch and feel. It's acting as a noun.
2. The word can also refer to an action, as in

    '*I book my theatre tickets through an agent.*'

3. In a phrase like 'book shelf' or 'book shop' the word is behaving as an adjective, giving more information about a noun ('shelf' and 'shop' respectively).

If you would like to find out more about word classes, you can find information on pp.61–72, and by using the index of this book.

(g)
1. The term 'Standard English' refers to 'that variety of English which is usually used in print and which is normally taught in schools, and to non-native speakers using the language' (LINC 1992, p.355). For more information, see p.53.
2. Accent refers to the ways in which speakers pronounce the sounds of English. Dialect refers to varieties of grammar and vocabulary.
3. There are no examples of non-standard grammar in this passage. (An example would have been if the writer had said '*I were twelve,*' where a single subject is sometimes followed, in some regional dialects, by a plural verb.)

Some of the vocabulary, however, would not be used in the same way in a standard English text. Examples are:

- 'Now then' as a sentence opening
- 'rising' thirteen
- 'our' Daniel
- 'Aye'
- 'a time of day eighty-three years back'.

Activity 5: word level work

(a) Among the points you might have chosen are the following:
1. The trees are personifed – they have 'fingers' which crack in the icy wind.
2. 'Crack' is an onomatopoeic word: that is, it conjures up the sound of the action it describes. This 'sound effect' is reinforced by having 'black,' a word with the same sound (an internal rhyme) in the previous line.
3. There's an effective comparison of the cattle with boulders, standing stock still in the icy fields. (This is an example of a simile.)
4. The breath of the cattle is vividly described as hanging 'in rags' (a metaphor).

I hope this small taste might have encouraged you to want to read the whole poem. You can find it, and a discussion of it, on pp.109–13. If you want to pursue the topic of figurative language (personification, similes and metaphors) you will find the index helpful.

(b) According to *Words Borrowed From Other Languages* by Sue Palmer and Eugenia Low (1998), a large format book ideal for KS2, the origins of the words are as follows:
1. chocolate: from the Aztec word 'xococatl' meaning 'bitter weather'.
2. tattoo: from a Tahitian word 'tatau' meaning 'mark'.
3. hubbub: from the Irish Gaelic 'hooboobbes,' a cry of victory.
4. lady: from the Old English 'hlaefdige' meaning 'a kneader of bread'.

You can find more comments on the excitement of words in Chapter 8.

(c) Segmenting words.
1. Segmenting words into phonemes or individual sounds is one of the most difficult of the 'splitting activities'. It's surprising how many adults can't do it easily, and for dyslexics it's extremely difficult. There are four sounds in 'bread' (b/r/e/d); 'b' and 'r' are known as a 'consonant cluster'. When the word is spoken, they come out very closely aligned, though they can each be distinguished if you listen very carefully. The 'e' and the 'a' on the other hand cannot be heard as separate sounds. They work as one to make the 'e' sound

you hear. This type of spelling, where two letters of the alphabet represent one vowel sound, is known as a vowel digraph. For more information, see pp.96–100.

2. In this group, you probably noticed this pattern:

    br ead
    h   ead
    l   ead
    d   ead

This is a family of words with the same 'rime' (the part of the word or syllable which contains the vowel and the final consonant or consonant cluster). The part of the word before the vowel (br, h, l, d,) is known as the onset. In a case like this, if children can gain instant recognition of this 'rime family' it will be of more help to them than splitting the words into individual sounds.

3. A morpheme is the smallest unit of meaning in a word. All of these words share one morpheme, 'lead', but others have been added to give a variety of meanings. The morphemes 'er', 'ing', and 's' are suffixes, because they have been added to the end of the word, and they change its grammatical function in each case. The morpheme 'mis' is a prefix, because it goes at the front of the word, and changes its meaning. Examples of prefixes and suffixes will crop up again and again in children's reading, and familiarity with them will also help their spelling if they learn to recognise them as groups of language features. For more on morphemes, see pp.91–2.

4. One syllable names include Ann, Jane, Tom, Ben. Those with two syllables include Peter, Charlie, Susan, Helen. Some three syllable names are Amanda, Christopher, Jennifer, Rhiannon.

Again, this splitting into syllables is a useful reading skill. Reading the names of animals, like 'giraffe' and 'monkey' is best tackled this way, at least as an initial strategy.

(d) You might have come up with 'e' as in 'cedar', or 'ey' as in 'keys', 'ee' as in 'meet' or 'ei' as in 'ceiling' or 'ie' as in 'field'.

English spelling is quite challenging for many children (and students!). Remembering the following points might help:
   – Some spellings are governed by grammatical rules (as in the suffixes we looked at in (c) 3 above. A good example is the past tense of regular verbs, which is always spelt -ed (though these don't all sound the same – compare 'wanted' and 'spoiled' and 'cropped').

- Understanding a prefix like 'tele...' or 'psych...' will open the door to spelling and understanding a whole family of words like 'psychiatrist' and 'psychology' and 'psychometric'.
- There are some spelling rules which, by continuous repetition, can help with such words as 'field' and 'ceiling' above.

You will find books to help with spelling in the Notes and the Bibliography of this book.

Notes

Some of my students are of the opinion that anything written before 1990 is not worth reading. Of course, it is true that thinking in education is changing very rapidly. However, there are certain texts which have become 'education classics'. When they were first published, they represented a radical shift in thinking which has formed a foundation for subsequent development. It would be a pity to dismiss them out of hand. You will find a few of these in the notes and in the bibliography.

Chapter 1

1 Any curriculum is only a selection of all the things that could conceivably be taught. As you read the National Curriculum programmes of study for English, it is interesting to ask yourself what else could have been included, or been given more space. There is very little mention of drama or media studies, for example, whereas a great deal of space is given to standard English. Why do you think this is?

The English National Curriculum has been through several revisions. In the form in which we now have it, there is nothing to explain the underlying rationale. The original version was put together by a committee chaired by Professor Brian Cox. You can read about what lay behind their thinking in *English for Ages 5 to 16* (1989). Chapters 15–17 set out their recommendations for attainment targets (now revised and renamed 'level descriptors') and programmes of study for English. Chapters 1–14 set out the rationale for their curriculum choices. The then Secretary of State for Education, Kenneth Baker, thought a rationale was unnecessary and only agreed that it should be included if it went at the back of the book. So this is one of the few examples of a book that starts at Chapter 15!

Brian Cox has also written two books which give further insights into how the National Curriculum for English was compiled and subsequently revised: *Cox on Cox* (1991) and *Cox on the Battle for the English Curriculum* (1995).

You may not wish to pursue the revisions to National Curriculum English in detail, but you should be aware that language knowledge, its selection and definition, whether we are talking about teachers' or children's knowledge, is a highly political issue and is likely to remain so for the foreseeable future (see Carter 1993).

2 If you would like to find out more about literacy targets, and the various initiatives in place to try to achieve these, the National Literacy Trust has a very informative web site: http://www.literacytrust.org.uk

The DfEE also has a useful web site: http://www.dfee.gov.uk/

3 The range of text types mentioned in the National Literacy Strategy includes the following:

- *Fiction*: stories with familiar settings; stories with predictable and repetitive patterns; traditional stories; stories from a range of cultures; stories about fantasy worlds; extended stories;

different stories by the same author; myths; legends; fables; parables; adventure and mystery stories; historical stories and short novels; stories that raise issues; stories by significant children's writers; classic fiction.

• *Plays*
• *Poetry*: nursery rhymes; chants; action verses; poems with familiar themes and settings; poems by significant children's poets; riddles, tongue twisters and humorous verse; nonsense verse; poems based on observation and the senses; shape poems; oral and performance poetry from different cultures and different times; poetry that plays with language, puns; poetry in a range of forms: haiku, cinquains, couplets, kennings, limericks, tanka, lists, thin poems, alphabets, conversations, monologues, syllabics, prayers, epitaphs, songs, rhyming forms and free verse, poems written as adverts, letters, diary entries, conversations; concrete poetry; longer classic poetry, including narrative poetry; choral and performance poetry.
• *Non-fiction*: signs; labels; captions; instructions, such as rules, recipes and texts showing how things are done; information books, including recounts of observations, visits, events; reports, including non-chronological examples; explanations of processes, systems, operations etc.; letters written for a range of purposes; articles and editorials in newspapers and magazines; adverts, circulars and flyers; leaflets to persuade, criticise, support, protest, object, complain; debates; biographies and autobiographies; diaries; journals; notices and public information documents; dictionaries and thesauruses, including IT sources; glossaries and indexes; directories; encyclopaedias.

If you are unsure where to start, a lot of help is available. There are, for example, several specialist journals. A particularly useful one is *Books For Keeps*, edited by Rosemary Stones. There are six issues a year and they offer student rates. They can be contacted at Books For Keeps, FREEPOST, 6 Brightfield Road, Lee, London SE12 8BR.

The National Grid For Learning is a very helpful source, especially the support offered for literacy in the Virtual Teachers Centre: http://vtc.ngfl.gov.uk/resource/literacy/index.html

4 You will find it interesting, in exploring these approaches to reading, to look at Chapter 1 of Margaret Meek's book, *On Being Literate* (1991).
5 Margaret Meek is also helpful in pursuing the idea of the reflective teacher of literacy in 'What do we know about reading that helps us teach?' in Carter (1990).
6 For further exploration of contrasts between old and new approaches to grammar teaching, see Carter, 'The new grammar teaching', in Carter (1990).

Chapter 2

1 For a useful overview of English language systems see Part I of Greene and Coulson's *Language Understanding. Current Issues* (1995).
2 A huge amount has been written on the teaching of literacy. A book which will help you to make links between language knowledge and literacy teaching is by Jeni Riley, *The Teaching of Reading: The Development of Literacy in the Early Years of School* (1996). Chapter 2 of that book offers a theoretical model for the process of reading. Most importantly for what I am saying in this chapter, it stresses the need to balance the contribution of 'top down' or 'meaning making' approaches and 'bottom up' or decoding approaches to reading and strongly emphasises the links between reading and writing.

The National Literacy Strategy Framework also emphasises the importance of combining text, sentence and word level strategies in the teaching of literacy. On p.9 it states: 'The range of strategies can be depicted as a series of searchlights, each of which sheds light on the text. Successful readers use as many of these as possible.'
3 The decontextualised teaching of aspects of English at text, sentence or word levels has rightly been frequently condemned as a waste of pupils' time, though large amounts of money continue to be spent on English language course books of all kinds. Many of the studies purporting to

show that there is no point in teaching grammar to children are referring to just this kind of decontextualised and frequently rote learning. In an interesting article, David Tomlinson (1994) reveals how flawed some of these studies are. In one school, for example, a group of pupils who, it was claimed, had had no grammar teaching and yet had shown considerable improvement – had actually benefited from two years' informal grammatical discussion of their written work with their teacher. This is exactly the kind of approach to grammar that one would hope to find: of course it requires delicate judgements to be made about what to make explicit and what to leave implicit in children's knowledge.

Chapter 3

1 For a summary of Bernstein's work and a useful discussion of some of its educational consequences, see Chapter 7 of *An Introduction to Language and Society*, by Martin Montgomery (1995).
2 You will find a very useful overview of theories of child language acquisition in Chapter 10 of *Understanding Children's Development*, by Peter K. Smith and Helen Cowie (1991).
  Another useful summary is in Garton and Pratt's *Learning to be Literate: The Development of Spoken and Written Language* (1989).
  Teaching Language and Literacy in the Early Years, by Godwin and Perkins (1998), is a very interesting and accessible text. As the title suggests, its main focus is classroom based, but they have helpful things to say about the processes of initial language learning and about the links between home and school.

Chapter 4

1 David Crystal (1988) defines a text as 'a set of sentences which cohere'. Section 73 of his book, *Rediscover Grammar*, is helpful if you would like to take your reading further. There are also detailed notes on cohesion in Wray and Medwell's *English for Primary Teachers. An Audit and Self Study Guide* (1997, p.36).
2 There is a useful section on 'The differences between spoken and written texts' in the *Language in the National Curriculum (LINC) Materials for Professional Development*. These can be obtained from the LINC secretary, Dept of English Studies, University of Nottingham, Nottingham NG7 2RO.
  The importance of teachers having a clear understanding of the differences between the grammars of speech and writing is the focus of Ron Carter's 'Standard Englishes in teaching and learning' (1994).
3 The National Writing Project was set up by the School Curriculum Development Committee in 1985. In the four years of its development and implementation phases hundreds of thousands of teachers and children participated in its work and many more have benefited from its findings. These are written up in a series of books published by Thomas Nelson, some of which are listed in the bibliography.
4 The London University Writing Research, undertaken by a team of people led by James Britton, was extremely influential in first drawing teachers' attention to the importance of defining a range of purposes and audiences for writing. This research explored children's writing development between the ages of 11 and 16. However, James Britton's ideas on the role of language in learning and thinking are of great importance for primary teachers also. You can read about these in his *Language and Learning* (1970).
5 There is an enormous amount of material published on genre theory. The Minibook Series published by the United Kingdom Reading Association (UKRA) offers concise introductions to some aspects of the research. In particular, see *Genres in the Classroom* by Alison B. Littlefair (1992) and *Exploring the Writing of Genres* by Beverly Derewianka (1996).

Another way in to this body of work is to read Kress and Knapp's 'Genre in a social theory of language' (1992). If you would like to go further than this, see the references to books by Derewianka, Kress, Littlefair and Martin in the bibliography.

Jonathan Culler, in *Structuralist Poetics* (1975, p.129), makes the interesting point that genres are not special varieties of language but sets of readers' expectations which allow the sentences of a language to become signs of different kinds to the reader. He is quite clear that genres are not fixed and that boundaries between what is perceived as one genre and another will change from age to age: 'change in modes of reading offers some of the best evidence about the conventions operative in different periods.'

For a critique of genre theory see Stratta and Dixon, 'The National Curriculum in English: does genre theory have anything to offer?' (1992). See also Myra Barrs, 'Genre theory. What's it all about?' (1995).

6   Though I do have some reservations about their apparent support for the idea of a fixed number of genres, I thoroughly recommend you to read Wray and Lewis, *Extending Literacy. Children Reading and Writing Non-Fiction* (1995). The book has very useful and practical things to say on extending children's skills beyond the 'basics' of literacy and in particular on helping them to interact with non-fiction books.

7   The way that genre theorists use the concept of register is founded on the functional theories of language proposed by Michael Halliday. A useful though very brief introduction to register can be found in *Exploring the Writing of Genres* by Beverly Derewianka (1996).

There are helpful comments on Halliday's concepts of field, tenor and mode in *Teaching About Language in the Primary Years*, by Rebecca Bunting (1997, p.14).

If you would like to take this topic further, see Halliday, *An Introduction to Functional Grammar* (1995).

Chapter 5

1   These approaches to reading were very much a part of the thinking of the Cox Committee and informed the chapters on reading in *English for Ages 5–16* (1989).

Margaret Meek's work is inspirational in exploring these approaches to reading. In addition to the two books I mentioned in the notes to Chapter 1, see also *Learning to Read* (1992) and *How Texts Teach What Readers Learn* (1988). See also Cairney, *Teaching Reading Comprehension* (1990).

There is a helpful chapter by Nick Jones, 'Reader, Writer, Text', in Carter (1990).

For interesting ways of interacting with texts at your own level (though they could also be adapted for the primary classroom) see Stibbs, 'The Teacherly Practice of Literary Theory' (1993). Don't be put off by the title, which sounds a bit daunting. Stibbs talks about how 'successful readers journey through a narrative, busy creating an imaginary world from verbal clues'. He has some stimulating ideas and suggestions on how to undertake these journeys.

Chapters 6 and 7

1   Help with grammar is available in a variety of formats and of course, levels of difficulty. I only have space to mention a small selection here. Two encyclopaedic volumes which are very accessible though definitely for dipping into only are Crystal, *The Cambridge Encyclopaedia of Language* (1987) and McArthur, *The Oxford Companion to the English Language* (1992).

Other books for 'dipping' are: Haegeman and Gueron, *English Grammar. A Generative Perspective* (1999); Akmajian *et al.*, *Linguistics. An Introduction to Language and Communication* (1995); Swan, *Practical English Usage* (1995). The LINC material mentioned in the notes to Chapter 4 has a helpful grammar section and a lot of useful material in the glossary.

At the rather 'heavy' end of the spectrum, but worth struggling with, are: Crystal, *Rediscover*

Grammar (1988); Gannon and Czerniewska, *Using Linguistics: An Educational Focus* (1980); Thorne, *Mastering Advanced Level English Language* (1997).

Living Language. Exploring Advanced Level English Language, by George Keith and John Shuttleworth (1997), provides interesting information, ideas and theory which will help you to read, listen and write in a more linguistically informed way. It is ideal for that linking of 'process' and 'systems' approaches to language which I have argued for in this book.

David Wray and Jane Medwell's book, *English for Primary Teachers: an Audit and Self Study Guide* (1997) is tailored to the needs of the ITT national curriculum. It is very condensed but extremely helpful.

At the 'popular' end of things are: Crystal, *Language from A–Z* (Books 1 and 2) (1991) (one is always reading in reviews how amusing and approachable certain books are: in the case of these two, this seems to me to be a very justifiable claim) and Barton, *Grammar Essentials* (1997). Crystal and Barton have collaborated in another very accessible book which has exercises and activities you can use to test your knowledge, *Discover Grammar* (1996). *English Grammar and Teaching Strategies: A Lifeline to Literacy,* by Joy Pollock and Elisabeth Waller (1999), is helpful both in supporting teachers' own language knowledge and in planning classroom based work.

2 This definition is taken from the LINC materials, which has a good section on 'Accent, dialect and standard English.'

There is a book by Trudgill which has become one of the 'education classics' I referred to above: *Accent, Dialect and the School* (1975).

3 It is not only those who speak the dialects of regions of Britain who may feel these insecurities. Irene Schwab (1994) gives some moving accounts of the feelings of those who speak a range of Creoles on arriving in Britain from the Caribbean. These are languages where the vocabulary is mainly drawn from English, French or another European language, but whose grammar and pronunciation patterns stem from African languages. Irene Schwab makes the point that 'Many students have retained the idea that the Creole languages they speak are not separate languages in their own right, but inferior versions of languages like English or French. This idea has been reinforced by the education systems both in the Caribbean and in Britain' (p.136).

4 See for example: Bryson, *Mother Tongue* (1990, Chapter 7), which is as readable and amusing as one would expect from Bill Bryson's other work; Cameron and Bourne, *Grammar, Nation and Citizenship: Kingman in a Linguistic and Historical Perspective* (1989); Crowley, *The Politics of Discourse: The Standard Language Question and British Cultural Debates* (1989); Doyle, *English and Englishness* (1989);   Lowe and Graham, *English Language For Beginners* (1998, Chapter 4).

5 You might find it useful to refer back to the chapter by Ron Carter (1994) which is referred to in the notes to Chapter 4.

6 If this is an aspect of language which interests you, you can read more about it in Chapter 1 of *English Language For Beginners*, by Michelle Lowe and Ben Graham (1998).

Chapter 8

1 The issue of priorities in language work with children takes us back yet again to one of my main arguments in this book, for teachers to have a clear view of text-based language learning which is rooted in a variety of contexts. Gordon Wells' research is absolutely central to illuminating the reasons why this approach works best. See previous references and also his 'Language as interaction' (1981).

2 One of the most important areas of language knowledge for primary teachers, especially in Key Stage 1, is that which explores the similarities and differences between home and school language. For a good overview of research in this area, see Edwards and Westgate, *Investigating Classroom Talk* (1994, pp.159–68).

Other useful readings are Willes, *Children Into Pupils* (1983) and MacClure and French, *A Comparison of Talk at Home and at School* (1981).

It's particularly important for teachers to gain insights into what the transition between home and school feels like for bilingual children. This is explored in *One Child, Many Worlds,* edited by Eve Gregory (1997).

3 Margaret Meek's books are very important in putting into words the wonder and excitement to be had from sharing the language of stories. See the notes for Chapters 1 and 5.

4 If you would like to do more reading on drama and language development, one useful book is *Learning Through Imagined Experience*, by Jonothan Neelands (1992).

5 The books mentioned in the notes for Chapters 6 and 7 will also be useful for further reading on the issues raised on pages 90 to 93 in this chapter.

6 For an interesting account of the uses of figurative language in everyday life, see *Metaphors We Live By*, by George Lakoff and Mark Johnson (1980).

7 For some helpful reading in this difficult area, and for much, much more, see *An Introduction to Language,* by Victoria Fromkin and Robert Rodman (1998).

8 / / around letters of the alphabet or phonetic symbols means that a sound is being referred to.

9 The word 'physical' has 7 sounds : /f/ /i/ /s/ /i/ /c/ /ə/ /l/
'frightened' also has 7 : /f/ /r/ /i/ /t/ /ə/ /n/ /d/
'transport' has 8 : /t/ /r/ /a/ /n/ /s/ /p/ /aw/ /t/
ə is a symbol known as a schwa in the international phonetic alphabet. It represents the central mid vowel which can be heard in these words, spoken with an RP accent.

10 Usha Goswami has highlighted the importance of work on onsets and rimes in the early years of reading. See 'Rhyme, analogy and children's reading', by Usha Goswami and Peter Bryant, (1992).

Chapters 9 and 10

1 If you would like to do more reading, particularly on how grammar can be studied in the context of a range of fiction and non-fiction texts, see *Grammar in Context*, by Geoff Barton (1999).

2 Some books to help you with text-based work in the classroom are: Carter, *Teaching Poetry in the Primary School* (1998); Lloyd *et al.* (eds), *The Literacy Hour and Language Knowledge* (1999); Mallett, M. (1992) *Making Facts Matter, Reading Non-fiction 5–11*; Powling and Styles, *A Guide to Poetry, 0–13* (1996).

Chapter 11

1 The National Literacy Trust provides a lot of useful information. The website is given in the notes to Chapter 1. You will find both literacy statistics and sources of information on gender and literacy on this website.

2 The research I am referring to here is the EXEL project (Exeter Extending Literacy). See Wray and Lewis (1997).

3 Throughout this book I have been concerned to stress that explicit language teaching *of the right kind* is likely to support children's reading, writing and speaking. For further thoughts on what this might mean, see Czerniewska, 'Learning about grammar' (1994).

Appendix 1

1 If you have not met this term before, in the specific sense in which it is being used here, you can find out what it refers to on p.29 of this book.

Bibliography

ACCAC (2000) *English in the National Curriculum in Wales.* Cardiff: HMSO.

Akmajian, A. *et al.* (1995) *Linguistics. An Introduction to Language and Communication,* 4th edn. Cambridge, MA: The MIT Press.

Atkinson, J. (1995) 'How do we teach pre-twentieth century literature?' in R. Protherough and P. King (eds) *The Challenge of English in the National Curriculum.* London: Routledge.

Bain, R. *et al.* (1992) (eds) *Looking into Language.* London: Hodder and Stoughton.

Barrs, M. (1995) 'Genre theory: what's it all about?', in B. Stierer and J. Maybin, (eds) *Language, Literacy and Learning in Education.* Clevedon: Multilingual Matters.

Barton, G. (1997) *Grammar Essentials.* Harlow: Longman.

Barton, G. (1999) *Grammar in Context.* Oxford: Oxford University Press.

Brice-Heath, S. (1983) *Ways With Words: Language, Life and Work in Communities and Classrooms.* Cambridge: Cambridge University Press.

Britton, J. (1970) *Language and Learning.* London: Allen Lane.

Britton, J. (1994) 'Vygotsky's contribution to pedagogical theory', in S. Brindley (ed.) *Teaching English.* London: Routledge.

Bromley, H. (2000) *Book-based Reading Games.* London: CLPE.

Bruner, J. (1983) *Child's Talk.* New York: Norton.

Bryson, B. (1990) *Mother Tongue.* London: Hamish Hamilton.

Bunting, R. (1997) *Teaching About Language in the Primary Years.* London: David Fulton Publishers

Byatt, A.S. (1985) *Still Life.* London: Chatto and Windus.

Cairney, T.(1990) *Teaching Reading Comprehension.* Buckingham: Open University Press.

Cameron, D. and Bourne, J. (1989) *Grammar, Nation and Citizenship: Kingman in a Linguistic and Historical Perspective.* London: Institute of Education.

Carter, D. (1998) *Teaching Poetry in the Primary School: Perspectives for a New Generation.* London: David Fulton Publishers.

Carter, R.(1990) ' The New Grammar Teaching,' in R. Carter (ed.) *Knowledge About Language and the Curriculum.* London: Hodder and Stoughton.

Carter, R. (1993) 'Proper English: language, culture and curriculum', *English in Education,* **27** (3) 3–14.

Carter, R. (1994) 'Standard Englishes in teaching and learning', in M. Hayhoe and S. Parker (eds) *Who Owns English?* Buckingham: Open University Press.

Christie, F. (1985) *Language Education.* Oxford: Oxford University Press.

Clegg, A.B.(ed.) (1964) *The Excitement of Writing.* London: Chatto and Windus.

Collins Gem (1997) *Spelling Guide.* London: HarperCollins Publishers.

Cox, B. (1989) *English for Ages 5 to 16.* London: HMSO.

Cox, B. (1991) *Cox on Cox.* London: Hodder and Stoughton.

Cox, B. (1995) *Cox on the Battle for the English Curriculum*. London: Hodder and Stoughton.

Crowley, T. (1989) *The Politics of Discourse: The Standard Language Question and British Cultural Debates*. London: Macmillan.

Crystal, D. (1987) *The Cambridge Encyclopaedia of Language*. Cambridge: Cambridge University Press.

Crystal, D. (1988) *Rediscover Grammar*. Harlow: Longman.

Crystal, D. (1991) *Language A–Z* (Books 1 and 2). Harlow: Longman.

Crystal, D. and Barton, G. (1996) *Discover Grammar*. Harlow: Longman.

Culler, J. (1975) *Structuralist Poetics*. London: Routledge and Kegan Paul.

Czerniewska, P. (1994) 'Learning about grammar,' in J. Bourne (ed.) *Thinking Through Primary Practice*. Buckingham: Open University Press.

de Bernières, L. (1994) *Captain Corelli's Mandolin*. London: Secker and Warburg.

Derewianka, B. (1990) *Exploring How Texts Work*. Rozelle, NSW: Primary English Teaching Association.

Derewianka, B. (1996) *Exploring the Writing of Genres*. Royston, Herts: UKRA.

DES (1975) *A Language For Life* (The Bullock Report). London: HMSO.

DES (1978) *Primary Education in England*. London: HMSO.

DES (1990) *English in the National Curriculum*. London: HMSO.

DES (1995) *Key Stages 1 and 2 of the National Curriculum*. London: HMSO.

DfEE and QCA (1999) *The National Curriculum. Handbook for Primary Teachers in England*. London: HMSO.

Dixon, J. and Stratta, l. (1999) *Writing Models, Genre Theories and the Future*. Unpublished.

Donaldson, M. (1978) *Children's Minds*. Glasgow: William Collins.

Doyle, B. (1989) *English and Englishness*. London: Routledge.

Edwards, A.D. and Westgate, D.P.G. (1994) *Investigating Classroom Talk*, 2nd edn. London: The Falmer Press.

Fromkin, V. and Rodman, R. (1998) *An Introduction to Language*, 6th edn. Orlando, FL: Harcourt Publishers.

Gannon, P. and Czerniewska, P. (1980) *Using Linguistics: An Educational Focus*. London: Edward Arnold.

Garton, A. and Pratt, C. (1989) *Learning to be Literate. The Development of Written and Spoken Language*. Oxford: Blackwell.

Godwin, D. and Perkins, M. (1998) *Teaching Language and Literacy in the Early Years*. London: David Fulton Publishers.

Goswami, U. and Bryant, P. (1992) 'Rhyme, analogy and children's reading', in P. Gough *et al.* (eds) *Reading Acquisition*. Hillsdale, NJ: Lawrence Erlbaum Associates.

Greene, J. and Coulson, M. (1995) *Language Understanding. Current Issues*, 2nd edn. Buckingham: Open University Press.

Gregory, E. (ed.) (1997) *One Child, Many Worlds. Early Learning in Multicultural Communities*. London: David Fulton Publishers.

Haegman, L. and Guéron, J. (1999) *English Grammar: A Generative Perspective*. Oxford: Blackwell.

Halliday, M. (1973) *Explorations in the Functions of Language*. London: Edward Arnold.

Halliday, M. (1985) *An Introduction to Functional Grammar*. London: Edward Arnold.

Holmes, J. (1992) *An Introduction to Sociolinguistics*. London: Longman.

Hudson, R. (1992) *Teaching Grammar*. Oxford: Blackwell.

Jones, N. (1990) 'Reader, Writer, Text', in R. Carter (ed.) *Knowledge About Language and the Curriculum*. London: Hodder and Stoughton.

Keith, G. and Shuttleworth, J. (1997) *Living Language: Exploring Advanced Level English Language*. London: Hodder and Stoughton.

Kress, G. (1982) *Learning to Write*. London: Routledge.

Kress, G. and Knapp, P. (1992) 'Genre in a social theory of language', *English in Education*, **26** (2) 4–15.

Lakoff, G. and Johnson, M. (1980) *Metaphors We Live By*. Chicago, Ill.: University of Chicago Press.

Lehmann, R. (1936) *The Weather in the Streets*. Glasgow: William Collins.

Lewis, C.S. (1969) 'On three ways of writing for children', in S. Egoff *et al.* (eds) *Only Connect*. Toronto, Oxford University Press.

Lewis, M. and Wray, D. (1996) *Developing Children's Non-fiction Writing*. Leamington Spa: Scholastic.

LINC (1992) Language in the National Curriculum Materials for Professional Development, unpublished. Obtainable from LINC Secretary, Department of English Studies, University of Nottingham, Nottingham NG7 7RO.

Littlefair, A. (1992) *Genres in the Classroom*. Royston, Herts: UKRA.

Littlefair, A. (1988) *Reading All Kinds of Writing*. Buckingham: Open University Press.

Lowe, M. and Graham, B. (1998) *English Language For Beginners*. New York: Writers and Readers Publishing.

Lock, A. (1980) *The Guided Reinvention of Language*. London: Academic Press.

Lloyd, P., Mitchell, H. and Monk, J. (eds) (1999) *The Literacy Hour and Language Knowledge*. London: David Fulton Publishers.

McArthur, T. (ed.) (1992) *The Oxford Companion to the English Language*. Oxford: Oxford University Press.

MacClure, M. and French, P. (1981) 'A comparison of talk at home and at school', in G. Wells, (ed.) *Learning Through Interaction. The Study of Language Development*. Cambridge: Cambridge University Press.

Mallett, M. (1992) *Making Facts Matter: Reading Non-fiction 5–11*. London: Paul Chapman.

Martin, J. (1989) *Factual Writing: Exploring and Challenging Social Reality*. New York: Oxford University Press.

Meek, M. (1988) *How Texts Teach What Readers Learn*. Stroud: Thimble Press.

Meek, M. (1990) 'What do we know about reading that helps us teach?', in R. Carter (ed.) *Knowledge About Language and the Curriculum*. London: Hodder and Stoughton.

Meek, M. (1991) *On Being Literate*. London: The Bodley Head.

Meek, M. (1992) *Learning to Read*. London: The Bodley Head.

Metcalfe, J. E. (1994) *The Right Way to Spell*. Kingswood, Surrey: Elliot Right Way Books.

Montgomery, M. (1995) *An Introduction to Language and Society*, 2nd edn. London: Routledge.

Murray, W. (1969) *Teaching Reading*. Loughborough: Wills and Hepworth.

National Centre for Literacy (1997) *The National Literacy Project Framework For Teaching*. Reading: National Literacy Centre.

National Writing Project (1989) *Audiences for Writing*. Surrey: Thomas Nelson.

Neelands, J. (1992) *Learning Through Imagined Experience*. London: Hodder and Stoughton.

Olson, D. (1984) 'See! Jumping! Some oral antecedents of literacy', in H. Goelman *et al.* (eds) *Awakening to Literacy*. Victoria, BC: University of Victoria.

Pinker, S. (1994) *The Language Instinct: the New Science of Language and Mind*. London: Allen Lane.

Plackett, E. (1998) 'Literacy landscapes', *The English and Media Magazine*, **38**, 4–8.

Pollock, J. and Waller, E. (1999) *English Grammar and Teaching Strategies: A Lifeline to Literacy*. London: David Fulton Publishers.

Powling, C. and Styles, M. (1996) *A Guide to Poetry 0–13*. Reading: University of Reading, Reading and Information Centre.

Riley, J. (1996) *The Teaching of Reading: The Development of Literacy in the Early Years of School*. London: Paul Chapman.

Roca, I. and Johnson, W. (1999) *A Course in Phonology*. Oxford, Blackwell.

Schwab, I. (1994) 'Literacy, language variety and identity', in M. Hamilton, D. Barton and R. Ivanic (eds) *Worlds of Literacy*. Clevedon: Multilingual Matters.

Sealey, A. (1996) *Learning About Language*. Buckingham: Open University Press.

Skutnabb-Kangas, T. and Cummins, J. (eds) (1988) *Minority Education: From Shame to Struggle*. Clevedon, PA: Multilingual Matters.

Smith, P.K. and Cowie, H.(1991) *Understanding Children's Development*, 2nd edn. Oxford: Blackwell.

Stibbs, A. (1993) 'The teacherly practice of literary theory', *English in Education*, **27**, (2) 50–8.

Stratta, L. and Dixon, J. (1992) 'The National Curriculum in English: does genre theory have anything to offer?', *English in Education*, **26** (2) 16–27.

Swan, M. (1995) *Practical English Usage,* 2nd edn. Oxford: Oxford University Press.

Thorne, S. (1997) *Mastering Advanced Level English Language*. Basingstoke: Macmillan.

Tomlinson, D. (1994) 'Errors in the research into the effectiveness of grammar teaching', *English in Education*, **28**, (1) 20–6.

TTA (1998) *Initial Teacher Training National Curriculum for Primary English* (annex C of DfEE Circular 4/98). London: DfEE.

Trudgill, P. (1975) *Accent, Dialect and the School*. London: Edward Arnold.

Trudgill, P. (1990) *The Dialects of England*. Oxford: Blackwell.

Vygotsky, L. (1962) *Thought and Language*. Cambridge, MA: The MIT Press.

Wells, G. (1981) 'Learning as interaction', in G. Wells (ed.) *Learning Through Interaction: The Study of Language Development*. Cambridge. Cambridge University Press.

Wells, G. (1987) *The Meaning Makers: Children Learning Language and Using Language to Learn*. London: Hodder and Stoughton.

Willes, M. (1983) *Children Into Pupils*. London: Routledge and Kegan Paul.

Wray, D. and Lewis, M. (1997) *Extending Literacy. Children Reading and Writing Non-fiction*. London: Routledge.

Wray, D. and Medwell, J. (1997) *English for Primary Teachers: An Audit and Self Study Guide*. London: Letts Educational.

Wray, D. and Medwell, J. (1998) *Teaching English in Primary Schools. A Handbook of Teaching Strategies and Key Ideas in Literacy*. London: Letts Educational.

Children's books

Allen, N. (1995) *The Queen's Knickers*. London: Red Fox, an imprint of Random House.

Biesty, S. and Platt, R. (1997) *Stephen Biesty's Incredible Everything*. London: Dorling Kindersley.

Brown, R. (1981) *A Dark Dark Tale*. London: Anderson Press.

French, V. and Wisenfeld, A. (1994) *Spider Watching*. London: Walker Books.

Goodhart, P. and Lambert, S. (1997) *Row Your Boat*. London: Picture Mammoth.

Grahame, K. (1908) *The Wind in the Willows*. London: Methuen Young Books.

Gribbin J. and Gribbin, M. (1994) *Time and Space*. London. Dorling Kindersley.

Harrison, M. and Stuart-Clark C. (1991) *A Year Full of Poems*. Oxford: Oxford University Press.

Hughes, T. (1963) *When the Whale Became*. London. Faber.

Lewis, C.S. (1950) *The Lion, the Witch and the Wardrobe*. Repr. 1980, London: HarperCollins.

Manning, M. and Granström, B. (1997) *Splish Splash Splosh! A Book About Water*. London: Franklin Watts.

Martin, R. (1990) *The First Lunar Landing*. Flinders Park, Australia: Era Publications.

Moore, E. and Grillet, S. (1999) *What's the Big Idea? Food*. London: Hodder Children's Books.

Palmer, S. and Low, E. (1998) *Words Borrowed From Other Languages*. Harlow: Longman.

Pearce, P. (1983) *The Way to Sattin Shore*. London: Viking Kestrel.

Pilcher, C. (1998) *The Time of the Lion*. London: Frances Lincoln.

Rowling, J.K. (1997) *Harry Potter and the Philosopher's Stone*. London: Bloomsbury Publishing.

Sendak, M. (1963) *Where the Wild Things Are*. London: The Bodley Head.

Sharratt, N. (1993) *Don't Put Your finger in the Jelly, Nelly*. Leamington Spa: Scholastic; A Picture Hippo.

Stickland, P. and Strickland, H. (1996) *Dinosaur Roar*. London: Puffin.

Theodorou, R. (1995) *When Dinosaurs Ruled the Earth*. Hove: Wayland.

Waddell, M. and Benson, P. (1992) *Owl Babies*. London: Walker Books.

Wilson, G. and Parkins, D. (1994) *Prowlpuss*. London: Walker Books.

Index